Things I Should Have Said

Things I Should Have Said

JAMIE LYNN SPEARS

WORTHY
PUBLISHING

New York • Nashville

Worthy
Hachette Book Group
1290 Avenue of the Americas, New York, NY 10104
worthypublishing.com
twitter.com/worthypub

First Edition: January 2022

Worthy is a division of Hachette Book Group, Inc. The Worthy name and logo are trademarks of Hachette Book Group, Inc.

The publisher is not responsible for websites (or their content) that are not owned by the publisher.

The Hachette Speakers Bureau provides a wide range of authors for speaking events. To find out more, go to www.hachettespeakersbureau.com or call (866) 376-6591.

All photographs included in insert are from the author's collection.

Print book interior design by Bart Dawson.

Library of Congress Control Number: 2021945912

ISBNs: 978-1-5460-0102-7 (hardcover), 978-1-5460-0100-3 (ebook), 978-1-5460-0166-9 (large print), 978-1-5460-0272-7 (Barnes & Noble signed edition), 978-1-5460-0271-0 (signed edition)

Printed in Canada

MRQ-T

10 9 8 7 6 5 4 3 2 1

For Maddie and Ivey
Being your Momma is my saving grace

Contents

A Letter from Jamie Lynn

Hi y'all,

I'd like to start by thanking you from the bottom of my heart for reading the story and events that make up my life so far. I feel honored and blessed to have a platform to share my words and truths. For most of my adult life, I have remained quiet and kept to myself out of respect for my own family and to protect the privacy of the ones I love. When I set out writing this book over a year ago, my main objective was to tell my story, in my own words, and share the events that have led me to where I am. I was so excited to share my experiences as a woman, an entertainer, a mother, a wife, and the product of being a child in the entertainment business. Now, I've done that and more, revealing never-before-heard stories of a young girl traversing family, fame, and the complexity that comes from growing up a Spears. Until recently I've tried to avoid the spotlight and speculation, hoping to preserve the privacy I genuinely cherish. During this writing process, there have been a lot of personal life events, over which I had no control, that affected the safety and well-being of me and my family. Others have spoken their truth and now I have been freed to share mine.

Writing has been cathartic and set me on a road of healing. My intention in sharing my story is to help others and convey love and compassion for things we still don't understand about each other. I only ask that people leave room and respect *my* truth, just as we have done for others. I am thankful for everyone who has been alongside me in this ever-changing journey that is my life. I'm still figuring it out, but it's time to finally say all the things I should have said a long time ago.

CHAPTER 1

The Business
of Family

The beginning of my story is well known. Like millions of babies all over the world, I was an oops. My momma and daddy were already the proud parents of Bryan, twelve, and Britney, nine, when I came along. Before I was born, money was tight for the family, and Daddy had taken to drinking—a lot and often. Momma owned and operated the Little Red School House, where her focus was childcare, not earnings. From what I can ascertain, these were lean times. With two healthy children and bills to pay, Momma and Daddy had decided not to have any more children.

But then Momma woke up one morning and didn't feel well. At first, she thought she was seriously ill, but after being examined, the doctor confirmed she was in fact pregnant, and already about seven weeks along. "That just can't be. My husband had a vasectomy." Momma left the doctor's office in disbelief. By the time she got home, Momma realized Daddy hadn't gone for his post-op checkup, and she was furious. "Jamie—I thought you took care to make sure this wouldn't happen. I walked around for days thinking I was really sick. And now I come to learn that you never went to make sure it took." Momma didn't talk to him for days, and she stayed mad for weeks. Daddy accepted another baby was joining the family. Momma just needed a little time to adjust to the idea of another baby at the time when Bryan and Britney were finally old enough to do a lot for themselves. My parents never considered aborting or giving me up for adoption. They were going to figure out how to make it work. Bryan and Britney were excited about having a sibling and everyone began to make plans.

On April 4, 1991, I came into the world and changed the fabric of my family forever. I didn't make it easy. After hours of labor, Momma was forced into an emergency C-section. I was a long and skinny baby but caught up in weight quickly. We became a party of five, and from what I've been told, I brought love and light into everyone's life. All of Momma's previous concerns about adding another child to her brood disappeared within hours of my arrival. As it turned out, I was a delightful baby who brought her so much joy and filled a void she never knew existed. I was the youngest by nine years, which meant I became everyone's baby, plaything, responsibility, and joy. Bryan and Britney were so excited to have a little sister. My siblings participated in just about every aspect of my early life. Bryan was a protective big brother and would occasionally feed and rock me. Britney became our momma's extra set of hands, and she did everything—bathing, feeding, playtime, and diaper changing. Both Bryan and Britney had their own lives to live, but they always made time for me. We were a loving but complicated family. I guess we still are.

Momma cared for me while my brother and sister went to school. I remember a lot of meals around the table and a lot of happy times when I was young. I was passed around a lot and doted on by everyone. I spoke early and entertained my family with my babbling, and my parents say my theatrical nature showed itself early. I chattered about anything, made funny faces, and was entertaining from toddlerhood onward. I had endless amounts of energy and ran around singing and dancing. Momma says I was smart, sweethearted, yet strong-minded. Daddy was often in and out. Momma was so busy with the three kids, she didn't have time to worry about what he was doing. When he was around, he spent much of his time in a chair trying to convince everyone else he wasn't drunk.

My memories of growing up in Louisiana are full of warm days in the sun and the craziness that comes with being a part of a boisterous family. Our family was big on togetherness and long on love. Family and friends filled our backyard every weekend. There was a large tree in the center of the yard that provided shade for the hours of playtime we all enjoyed. When she could, Momma made lots of food, and there was usually a grill sizzling. People would stop by throughout the day, which was typical of life in Louisiana. Many afternoons were spent with neighbors and friends. We would play outdoors, ride go-carts, and swim in our neighbor's pool. But from early on, with Daddy's struggles and the discord between my parents, I could see that there was something different about my family. It would be several years before I would be able to identify just how different we were from other families.

Anyone who knew us before all the fame would tell you we had a modest home in Kentwood. The town of Kentwood is small; everyone says good morning to each other by name or asks, "How y'all doin'?" It's the type of place where everyone knows each other's business, and people are nosy. But don't cross a local because we protect our own.

My favorite memories from growing up are of all of us around a table together eating Momma's cooking. She made RO*TEL chicken, peas, and mashed potatoes, crabs—you name it. We all loved her country cooking, but Daddy and Bryan boiling up shrimp and crawfish was a family favorite. Sometimes when people asked if there was extra, she had to answer no. Momma couldn't risk sharing what little food there was. During periods when money was scarce, Momma learned to make do with what she had. Some nights she would feed my siblings and me first. Then she would eat whatever we left behind.

In my early years, I was the princess. No matter how their lives were changing, Bryan and Britney made me feel special, and they loved me despite my mischievousness. Bryan came to my school one day and spoke to my kindergarten teacher. He said, "How's she doing here?" The teacher replied, "Jamie Lynn is one of our best and best-behaved students." Bryan laughed. "This one? No way. She can never sit still!" It seemed early on I knew my audience.

We were a typical family who spent hours amusing ourselves with silly challenges and one-upping each other in fun. The fame and money came later, but it wasn't like that when I was young. As a young girl, I never thought about how much money we had or worried about whether we had enough. My siblings and I didn't suffer, but looking back, I can see that the instability in our lives led to periods of financial difficulties. Somehow, we always had what we needed, but I knew better than to ask for anything expensive. I learned that lesson early on, when Momma and her friend took me shopping. Momma's card didn't go through at Limited Too, and her friend had to pay for my clothes. The concern in Momma's eyes belied her reassurances that everything was fine. To this day, I can still remember the sting of humiliation.

My daddy was well known for developing businesses and was good at every job he took on. He worked in construction and welding. He also had a seafood restaurant called Granny's, known for crawfish and shrimp. At some point he gave it to Bryan, who eventually sold it. Daddy even opened the first gym in our area, and it was a big hit. I remember my sister taught classes there too. Eventually big business came to Louisiana and the gym closed.

He spent years working as a welder and a boilermaker. He did whatever he needed to do to support the family the best way he knew how.

At times, the stress of providing for us led him down a nasty path. He spent years in a cycle of bad behavior. Daddy never really stopped drinking, but sometimes he took breaks. It was the time between jobs that affected him the most, and that's when he would start drinking a lot. Stories of his drinking are family lore. One of the crazier ones happened before I was born. The whole family gathered to take my great-granny Lexie to the Pizza Hut for her birthday. She loved Pizza Hut. Momma worked all day but made an effort to get herself and my siblings dressed nice for the celebration. The family waited on Daddy, who finally came swaggering in, intoxicated. He couldn't string sentences together and tried to slur, "I'm not drunk." Momma was fuming mad. Everyone took two steps away from Momma because they could sense something was about to happen. Uncle Austin was unloading the work truck and Momma said, "Get that ice chest down from there!" He placed it in front of a tree and backed away slowly as Momma, all dressed up and looking pretty, stomped around to the back of the house, grabbed a shotgun, and shot up that ice chest. The family just stared as she destroyed the cooler. But Daddy still claimed he wasn't drunk.

Daddy thought he was a good drinker and that no one could tell when he was inebriated. But the funny thing was, his entire countenance gave him away. The minute his foot would start tapping, you knew he was itching for a drink and was about to leave us for a while. The way Momma explained it was by saying, "Sometimes things just get to be too much for him, and he takes off." As if that explanation made any sense to a child. Momma tried protecting him with her excuses and tried to keep us kids from seeing him drunk. And as a young child, I didn't understand how his behavior affected everyone else. I just felt like something wasn't right. Still, he was my daddy, whose time and attention I craved. He spent most of my life in that cycle of ruinous behavior. His bouts of drinking always caused me periods of torment and sorrow. It would be many years before I could acknowledge and address the seeds of resentment—at Daddy for his drinking and at Momma for how she managed her life—that were planted during this time.

Momma worked hard to keep everything together and take care of us. The fact that Britney was much older made things a little more manageable. She pitched in whenever Momma needed help. Britney took on the responsibility of cleaning and dressing me, and she dedicated herself to making me look perfectly adorable every time. Momma was grateful to have Britney and acknowledges my sister was much better than she was at the girlie things. I grew up feeling like I had two mothers. Bryan would look after me when needed, and once Britney's career started to take off and Momma started to travel with her for work, his responsibilities doubled. Sometimes Daddy was around, but my relationship with him started to collapse as I grew. I just never knew what version of Daddy would appear, and that made it hard.

I came into the world with a big personality and learned early how to get attention. Everyone's response to my antics only made me want more attention and I did anything I could to hold on to the spotlight. Sometimes I would imitate someone or sing a song. Music was always playing in our home. Early on, I watched and listened to my sister singing and making up dance routines for fun. I wanted to get in on the act whenever I could, and I'd try to mimic my sister. My whole family got a kick out of me being outrageous. When I couldn't get attention that way, I would create mischief. I loved to hide. It was a surefire way to get everyone to focus all of their energy on me. Eventually I'd come out of hiding and the array of responses—relief, disbelief, and anger—made me laugh.

One time Momma took us to a store, and I decided to hide in the racks of clothes. I was so tiny, no one noticed me. After several minutes, I made myself known and everyone sighed in relief. From that day forward, Momma made sure someone always had an eye on me. Other times I would say the most outrageous things. Momma held her breath many times waiting to see what would come out of my mouth in public. How I loved to make her cringe! But I made certain Daddy wasn't around for my pranks. He wouldn't tolerate that type of behavior.

By the time I entered first grade, our family was experiencing a metamorphosis. Bryan was a young adult planning his next step, and Britney was about to become a household name.

My sister was a natural talent, whose approachable manner and attractiveness ensured she was going to be successful in the entertainment industry. She worked hard at developing her talent, and at fifteen Britney had already built an impressive résumé. Her music demo convinced recording executives at Jive Records to give her a chance. Momma and Daddy were delighted all the hard work was starting to pay off. Like my sister, I was enrolled in dance and voice lessons. My sassiness and dramatic nature naturally led me toward acting. Momma and Daddy made sure I was given all the same opportunities as Britney to develop my talent. My sister was my role model. She wasn't just full of talent; Britney had an ease about her onstage that I yearned to emulate. I never wanted her career or to follow in her footsteps, only to harness her confidence and magnetism. Some people have suggested Britney's performance prowess unconsciously swayed me to focus on acting, but my affinity for portraying characters had started at such a young age, it was more like acting chose me.

My sister's rise to fame brought profound changes to our family dynamics. Momma and Daddy knew that Britney's long-term success was a long shot, but they were going to do everything possible to get her in front of the right people, build the proper team, and ensure she was compensated accordingly. It was a plan that worked because of the luck that accompanied Britney's hard work and talent. As deals were made, the family dynamics shifted. Britney had a dream, and that dream was going to affect all of us. Although she remained unaffected early on, my sister's life became more demanding as her notoriety grew. Everyone made sure her needs were met, and we all became responsible for helping her as she reached a greater level of success. We needed to keep her happy and productive. I was so young as she emerged on the world stage that I didn't notice how things had begun to change. My parents always expected me to do as I was told. At first, that didn't seem unusual in the parent-child dynamic. But I was taught to defer to Britney or behave in a way that made things easier for her. Momma said stuff like, "Come on, Jamie Lynn, we don't want to upset your sister." It could be something as simple as "Let Britney do that first," or "If it's good for your sister, it's good for all of us." What complicated things even more was that Momma reveled in the attention that came with being Britney's mother. People were more interested in who she was than ever before, and I think she loved that part of it.

Daddy's intermittent stays in the house never ceased to confuse me. He took an interest in everything we did. Daddy insisted upon greatness in anything we dedicated ourselves to achieving. I think it was hard for Bryan because he wasn't the star athlete Daddy wanted him to be. Through it all, Momma continued with her stern manner of parenting me, but it felt as if she had a different set of standards for my older siblings.

When we weren't out on tour or managing the business, we would return home to just be a family. I loved going on tour as long as I was with my family or could bring a friend along, but I preferred being home. At home, Momma returned to the kitchen, and we were just kids. For a couple of years, we all went to school. Life really was normal for us. When Daddy wasn't drinking, things were a little better. Once in a while we would shoot hoops or toss a ball around. He was my armchair quarterback in all things and had advice and opinions on everything. He and Momma had worked hard to get my sister's career going, and he was certain he knew how I needed to go about things. Even when we disagreed, that version of Daddy was tolerable. The things I loved about him made the disappointment and anger that came with his neglect and absences all the harder. I was often left to deal with these emotions on my own. My brother and sister, already teens by this point, had friends and freedoms that helped them to escape.

Since Momma was an actual educator, she took it upon herself to teach Britney how to drive. Momma took her out a few times and eventually felt it was safe enough for me to come along. My sister was fifteen at the time and didn't have her license yet. She was driving the black four-door Lexus with a gray stripe that was Momma's treasure. Momma adored that car, even though it had come to her after a wreck. The car ran hot all the time, but to us it was so much nicer than our previous cars. Britney was driving the Lexus down the road and let the car drift over the center line. Another car came into our lane and Momma had to grab the wheel suddenly to avoid a collision. No one wore seat belts back then, and I was flopping around like a fish on dry land. Britney and Momma were screaming nonsensical words as the car swayed and careened right into a ditch. One after another, we shouted, "I'm fine!" Thinking quick, Momma changed places with Britney. We all knew Daddy would have a fit if he found out Britney was driving during the crash. This was not the first time Momma tried to keep Daddy unaware of all the facts.

But Momma told us she did it because she was afraid the insurance issues would be made worse if an underage driver was at the wheel. All the effort we put into keeping Daddy from losing his temper made me uneasy. I was too young to understand the complexities of their marriage, but I was wise beyond my years. Momma always cared more about Daddy's feelings than doing the right thing. In her way, she was trying to maintain stability and keep the peace. Momma often put us in a difficult position rather than confronting the situation head-on. We all pretended—said things or stayed quiet, as Momma asked—to make sure Daddy was placated and their relationship remained intact. Daddy was on "a strictly need to know basis." It was easier to manage by letting him come and go as he wished. The concept of "need to know" expanded way beyond Daddy. As the family of an emerging pop star, we all had to learn how to manage information and secrets in a protective manner. Our family, just like so many others, cared, protected, and supported each other to the exclusion of everything else—sometimes even ourselves. Momma's indoctrination into this way of living was circumstantial, but Daddy's childhood experiences forced him to adopt this philosophy as a protective mechanism. We protect each other at all costs.

Learning about my father's childhood helped me understand him better. Daddy's upbringing was difficult. My grandfather, Paw-Paw June, was a physical man who used his hands to solve problems. Maw-Maw Jean was a good woman in a difficult situation. In those days women didn't leave their husbands. When Daddy was fourteen, his baby brother died, and soon after so did his mother. Paw-Paw June eventually married Maw-Maw Ruth, but Great-Granny Lexie, Jean's mother, took part in raising Daddy too. Despite the women's efforts, my father was raised by an abusive father who made unreasonable demands of his son in all aspects of his life. Daddy was forced to practice sports for hours at a time—past the point of exhaustion. For basketball, Paw-Paw June made Daddy shoot one hundred shots after practice. Daddy loved basketball, but his father made him abandon the court for the football field. He followed his father's directive to play college football, knowing all along he would have been much more impactful as a basketball player.

Momma's people were a completely different sort. Momma's mother came to America from Europe as a war bride who married a Louisianan. Her family had money and were refined and artistic. Music and art were a large part of her experience. Momma makes no claims to talent, but I remember loving to listen to her play the piano and sing in the church choir. My parents were high school sweethearts who stayed together and fell deeper in love. Momma's love for Daddy was a powerful force and Daddy's was just different. His love ebbed and flowed as the years passed. The diversity of their experience and marriage created a dynamic mix of passion, talent, and unrelenting determination. As their children, we are the embodiment of their ambitions and hopes, yet driven by our respective dreams and purpose.

The turmoil of my parents' marriage took a back seat to the

growth and management of my sister's stardom and my developing career. They continued to work together regularly and made unified decisions, even well after they finally divorced in 2002. After the split, Daddy was still in and out of the house all the time. Family relationships are complex, after all. For years, my family has always had the uncanny ability to show up and have a meal together, even if we are struggling with one another. Somehow, we managed to put our grievances aside. The philosophy so inherent to being a Spears has always been, *When everything is said and done, we are a family. We may not like or even love each other in a given moment, but odds are it will pass, and we'll find our way back.* We have carried on this way for decades. But as I matured, the demands on me to pretend that everything was fine forced me to sacrifice my own needs.

CHAPTER 2

My Rising Star and *All That*

Momma tells me she knew the minute I started talking that I was a natural-born performer. Having a large family and lots of people around guaranteed I always had an audience. There's just something about getting a response from other people that I've always loved. I would come bounding into the room twirling and shaking my hips. Once I captured someone's attention, I just let my imagination take over and performed whatever antics came to mind. As the baby, just about everyone humored me. I loved to sing too, and as I got older, I created variety skits that showcased all of my meager talents. By the time Britney's first single was released, I was dreaming about becoming an actress. Momma and Daddy agreed to send me to voice and dance lessons, got me headshots, and supported me. The dream of being a performer was always mine, and in no way did I feel my parents were living vicariously through me. I practiced diligently and relished receiving accolades from everyone. Singing was only part of what I loved about performing. My sister's voice was throaty and strong, while mine was fluid and controlled. People said we were different but equally as talented. But my true love was acting.

As Britney's fame grew, it caused a lot of strain on the family. Britney's career took her far from home and oftentimes Momma traveled with her. I could tell Momma was disconcerted by Daddy's unreliability, and she exhausted herself keeping everything afloat. The periods of neglect and disregard for Momma's needs led to frustration. I think so much energy was directed to keeping my sister's career moving that my parents neglected to pay attention to each other. Momma's anger and disappointment escalated as demands on her time increased. I was the only kid still at home, but I wasn't the only one who noticed. We all felt the stress. Britney finally said, "Momma, if you leave Daddy, I will buy you a house." That promise came just at the right time. For as long as Momma could, she tried to carry on with how we lived our lives. In Louisiana, she was determined to maintain her Southern ways, which included inviting friends and neighbors in and chatting with friendly folks. But

Britney's fame changed all that. People started to drive by or walked around the property. Over time there were more and more bizarre incidents of strangers approaching the house. Some people would come up to the windows and peek inside just to get a glimpse of Britney's bedroom. It happened at all hours. The illusion of safety ended one night when a man pulled up in a white van just outside our house. I yelled, "Momma, there's someone parked outside and watching the house." We had no idea how long he had been out there or what his intentions were, but we weren't taking any chances. The scene was creepy. Momma and I locked ourselves in the bathroom and called Rob, one of Britney's security staff, who stayed on the phone with us until the police arrived. Soon after, we were living in a new house that provided a more secure environment for me and Momma. For added safety we got two pedigreed German shepherds that were *actually* from Germany. We flew out to California to meet the dogs, Roby and Ory, to make sure we were all compatible. They were the best, most loyal dogs, and I think they would have killed to protect us.

Daddy didn't live with us in the new house, but he'd show up whenever he wanted, and Momma carried on as she always had and let him in. For Momma, leaving Daddy was one thing. Staying away was a completely different story. She would justify his visits by saying, "Jamie Lynn. He's still your father." Their dynamic added to my own complex feelings about him. I just couldn't rely on him to be the dad I needed. Observing how my parents said one thing but did something else undermined my ability to trust them.

Perhaps my love of playing characters stems from a desire to abandon my stressors and escape to other worlds. Anytime I quieted my thoughts to take on another persona, I felt transformed. The freeing sensation only added to my enjoyment. I improved my talent by infusing fun into everything I created. The hours I spent developing characters helped me form a clearer view of my future. I always sought out ways to get in front of an audience. School plays, church performances, and even local auditions served as my training ground. I took whatever parts I could get. I played one of the orphans in *Annie*, performed in many church productions, and added singing to my dance recitals. Creative outlets were limited in my small town, and I was forced to manufacture my own opportunities. Momma was opposed to me competing in our school's beauty pageant, claiming she didn't want me to be a part of anything that has girls solely judged on looks. I shot some print ads and auditioned for a few commercials. I shot national commercials for Clorox and Pepsi. The dream necessitated that I do anything that provided an outlet for my creativity and added to my résumé.

The entire family was soon involved in the business of Britney's career. Bryan discovered that practical, hands-on learning was easier than classroom instruction. He was taken under the wing of Britney's management team to learn the basics of brokering deals and managing people. This led into the touring years, where the family traveled with Britney in support. It was the best way for us to stay close as a family. I was still so young and really enjoyed when we were all together. Although I preferred being home in Kentwood, touring with my sister provided a built-in audience for my own performances. Momma always encouraged me to bring a friend for part of the long-haul tours. We would spend time developing mini performances and characters, filling the hours of free time refining our act. The crew for the shows was massive, and everyone granted me their attention whenever I went into character or did an impersonation. They said, "Jamie Lynn, you're a natural!" During preparations for the show, I ran around backstage and hung out. Watching Britney perform was inspiring. Sometimes I'd watch from the side stage or sit in the audience. How she managed to capture the attention of thirty thousand people at once on a nightly basis baffled me. She always experienced an adrenaline spike, followed by exhaustion when she was done. But her smile of gratification remained. At times it was unsettling how drained she was after a show, especially as the tour reached its fourth or fifth month. Between her schedule, rehearsals, and performances, I could see how profoundly the exhaustion was affecting her.

After the long day of setup, staging, and performing, the buses were loaded up to go to the next stop. This was my time to shine. With my sister's encouragement, sometimes with a friend, I would jump into character and entertain everyone on the bus. Britney would throw out suggestions and everyone would urge me to do more. These one- and two-man shows were the basis of the characters I eventually brought to television. Occasionally, someone recorded these informal performances, and I loved to watch them over and over again. Momma and Britney provided so much encouragement that I developed the confidence to dream bigger.

Watching my sister own the stage, being Britney, taught me something about myself. I realized I was more interested in the chameleonlike effect of becoming someone else and creating a character so different from myself. Still, eliciting a response from an audience, no matter how I did it, always thrilled me, and I loved comedy. Comedic timing is like having rhythm. I aspired to become a great comedic actor after spending hours watching actors like Drew Barrymore, Tina Fey, Jimmy Fallon, and just about everyone on *SNL*.

For a couple of years my life went back and forth between living in Kentwood and traveling on my sister's tours. Each time I returned home to Louisiana, I resumed my typical kid existence and kept working on my acting and performing. I just kept at it. Then I got a lucky break. A production assistant from Nickelodeon watched a video of me performing my characters in some behind-the-scenes footage from my sister's tour. Whatever she saw prompted a meeting with my team, and I was asked to audition to join the cast of the Nickelodeon sketch comedy show *All That*. I was sent sides, which were short skits I would perform live in front of a team of producers. This was before the era when high-resolution videos or phone recordings were used to seek talent. They also requested I come prepared with one of my own character skits. I chose Louise McGillicutty, a character I'd created while on tour with my sister. Louise, who was later renamed Thelma Stump, was a combination of my great-granny Lexie and Rob, one of Britney's security guards.

I went into the studios to an audition room, where several executives observed and made the final decision on hiring me. I was so nervous, but as soon as I got into character, the pure fun of it took over. They would throw lines at me, and I would ad-lib in a way that showcased my abilities. Once I was finished, they said, "We'll be in touch soon." I went home and waited for the call. It didn't take more than a couple of days. Hearing I was hired was one of the coolest moments in my life. I was so excited. This was the kid version of *Saturday Night Live*, a show that is basically responsible for my love of sketch comedy. *All That* had been on hiatus for a little over a year, and I was going to be part of a new cast.

By the time the contracts were signed and the cast was assembled, I had just turned eleven. *All That* had a long summer shoot in LA. When we started shooting, Mom and I flew out to California with my dog Izzy and stayed in the home Britney shared with Justin Timberlake in Hollywood. The area had a great vibe, but I was so busy working I barely had time to enjoy it. When filming, time evaporates quickly. As the sister of a newly minted pop icon, and with my own growing fame, security had to be considered whenever I went out and about. In light of Britney's media coverage, the paparazzi were always in hot pursuit of a Spears story. Occasionally, I went out anonymously. But as much as I loved it, all of my friends back home were moving on with their own lives and having experiences I wasn't a part of, and at times I was conflicted.

My efforts to showcase my talent were paying off, and yet a part of me still yearned to be home. With all the travel and work, my love of being home, a peaceful place where I could relax, continued to be my preference. We would shuttle back and forth between California and Louisiana as much as the schedule would allow. Unfortunately, the constant travel and demands on my time made it impossible to care for Izzy, and I had to give her away. Sometimes I would get to take care of one of Britney's dogs when I was missing having one of my own.

My shooting schedule for the show created more havoc in our family. Britney and Bryan were absorbed in their own projects, which provided Momma the time to be with me in California. I think over the years my parents developed a power struggle that intensified as my sister, and then I, became successful. Our foray into the entertainment world thrust my parents into roles they had to learn in real time. As we became working performers, there wasn't a class or seminar series for Momma and Daddy. The lines of parenting were blurred by the demands of our jobs, and decisions had to be made for both my sister and me. This took a toll on their relationship. We went from a humble Louisiana family to world notoriety in a matter of months. It became painfully obvious that my parents' marriage was failing, and I couldn't do anything to make it right. I knew things were bad between them, but at least I escaped the embarrassment of them being divorced. I feared the changes a divorce would bring. I was mostly concerned with how things were going to change day to day. As a young girl, I didn't want to split weekends, sacrifice time with friends, or change my life. Momma hoped that it would change her relationship with Daddy and our new home would provide a more stable environment.

In the end, all of the drama and the divorce were a waste anyway. Britney's house gesture was in vain. After we moved, Daddy still showed up whenever he wanted, and Momma simply let it happen. All that for nothing. Unfortunately, it didn't take long for his drinking to take hold and erode the fragile nature of our relationship. The expectation that Daddy would continue to love me and be what I needed dissolved over time.

This was a difficult period in my life. I came to resent the very man I wanted to adore. The years of yearning for Dad to love me as I needed slowly turned to disdain. I always wanted to have Dad in my life, but never knowing if he was drinking caused me profound anxiety. Much of that anxiety was a result of Momma not doing what she should have done to protect me when he was on a bender. Daddy's behavior and Momma's enabling denied me essential moments of my life. We stopped communicating, and yet, and much to my dismay, he would show up in our apartment in California or on set. During the months I lived in Kentwood, he'd come to my basketball games. Whether he was drinking or not, I couldn't trust what condition he may have been in. At times, I suggested to my mom to not tell Daddy about my games. Tormented, I repeatedly asked that he not come to my events. Just the idea that he would appear was enough to cause me distress. It was so much more than just the embarrassment his actions may have caused; the anxiety interfered with my focus, and I couldn't foster the talent I felt was in me.

The holidays were particularly difficult times for my family. We would all be together, but there was an underlying tension that affected everyone. Momma did all she could to suppress the uneasiness. She would spend hours filling the house with her cooking and trying to create a festive atmosphere. We learned to pretend that everything was just fine. Invariably every holiday ended up the same. Daddy would get to a point where he couldn't "deal with all of it," and leave. It always tore me apart, and I knew I would feel the sting of that pain for many years. I remember saying to myself, "I will not do this to my children." I never had a good Christmas until my first one with my daughter Maddie.

My work on *All That* was my saving grace. Although I loved the consistency daily life in Louisiana provided—school, activities, and friends—my work guaranteed that I traveled to California for the summers to film. Performing was liberating in many ways, and allowed me to focus on something other than my family struggles. As my siblings and I continued to work and create, Daddy finally sought out the help he needed and attended a rehab in California. At the time, this helped me settle into my work and enjoy my experience.

Each time, I arrived to shoot a new season full of anticipation and excitement. But as a fickle preteen, I also experienced bouts of melancholy and a yearning for home. I became adept at hiding these feelings and focused on my work. The Spears family trait of masking emotions to get through the days was deeply engrained in my psyche.

Days on the set of *All That* were fun, but the experience also served as a master class in comedy. Oddly enough, when I arrived on set for the first week, I was shy, almost intimidated. The reality of performing on a nationally broadcast show was settling in. For my first appearance, my one job was to come down a slide dressed as an elf and giggle. The director said, "Action," and I froze. I couldn't do it. Momma stood at the side stage and gave me a look that said, *After all of the work you did to get here...now this?* But the cast was nurturing and encouraging, and within minutes I calmed my nerves and pulled it off. Later, when we shot the opening sequence for the show, the cast made me feel like one of the team. Within weeks I settled in and found my footing.

We were an ensemble cast, which diminished the level of pressure I might have otherwise felt. My castmates and I shared the responsibility of ensuring the show's success. Honestly, it was the most fun I have ever experienced performing. Weekly we would create characters and reuse ones the audience loved. I learned to get out of my comfort zone by playing characters who felt foreign to me. The show always had a guest star cameo or a musical performer. Justin Timberlake, former cast member Nick Cannon, and even my sister made cameos. The list of musicians included just about every popular band or singer in the nineties—Destiny's Child, LL Cool J,

Usher, the Spice Girls, and the Backstreet Boys. We had an elaborate greenroom that appeared on-screen for the viewers, where the cast and guests would hang out. *All That* was a four-camera-shot show, which allowed for us to rehearse Monday through Wednesday and shoot live on Thursday and Friday. The week would start with a table read, where writers would take notes and make changes. After the meeting, rehearsals would start. If I wasn't rehearsing, I'd have costume fittings, hair and makeup sessions to help create the characters I'd be playing. By the time we started filming, we were all pumped up to get into costume and perform in front of the live audience. The level of adrenaline was palpable on those days. As an ensemble, not everyone is in every skit. When we weren't on-screen, the cast hung out in the greenroom with the guest performers. We'd get to see everyone perform, meet the musicians, and have fun.

The writers would create characters and often ask us for input. Sometimes I would act out a written concept and be asked to add my own spin to it. I loved when the writers took a liking to a particular character I'd created, like Thelma Stump, and wrote her into the show. Becoming an active part of the process was validating and encouraged me to create more characters. Some of my favorite skits from the show include "Thelma Stump," "Trashin' Fashion," and "Know Your Stars." "Know Your Stars" was when one of the *All That* stars sat on a chair center stage and a voice-over would share falsehoods about them. My favorite time was when I got snippy with the voice-over and hurt his feelings. Of course, I apologized, and he resumed spouting silly lies no one would ever believe.

During the early 2000s, when *All That* was shot, Nickelodeon had requirements about continuity—no changes to our appearance were allowed. During a shoot, I lost one of my front teeth. I couldn't have a tooth in one shot and a gap in the next. Someone said, "We've got to get a flipper"—an attachable temporary tooth. By the next morning I was back on set with my flipper in place and finished the scene.

All That had a huge fan base. Our show slid into SNICK House, the Saturday night block created by Nickelodeon to attract mid- to older teens. The block was hosted by former *All That* castmate Nick Cannon. A few times I took part in *On-Air Dare*, Nickelodeon's version of *Fear Factor* that aired during SNICK. I had to attempt to drink five gallons of blue cheese dressing, be doused in eggs, and eat "earwax tacos," all in the name of entertainment. A fun fact about *On-Air Dare* is that some of the substances used in the challenges are not what they appeared to be. If you've seen the blue cheese dressing challenge, it was diluted for easier consumption. The eggs on set were actually peaches. Even the infamous slime is made of vanilla pudding and food coloring. Producers needed to ensure the safety of the cast by avoiding the use of allergenic foods and materials. Sometimes they would have two stars from different shows compete against each other to draw a larger audience. The executives at Nickelodeon did a great job of weaving their performers into various programs and bringing new faces into their programming. The producers of *All That* were determined to diversify Nickelodeon and showcase talents from a cast that had different experiences and backgrounds. The show received a number of awards, and several cast members went on to star in their own television shows. After spending a few seasons on the show, I felt a growing confidence in my abilities as an actress and began to think about what might come next. Producer and writer Dan Schneider, who'd created *All That*, recognized my talent. He went on to develop many other projects and ultimately was the driving force behind my opportunity to get a starring role in my next job.

CHAPTER 3

Teenage Angst

When my Nickelodeon contract started, I was so excited about getting to do what I loved, and I was most certainly grateful, but being away from home so much left me bereft. As much as I enjoyed being on television, I also loved being home and living like an average tween. Momma kept me humble, and most of the kids at home treated me as they always had—I was just Jamie Lynn. There were others who tried to become my friend because of my fame and some who razzed me for it. Fortunately, my good friends remained steadfast, and have stayed that way even now.

Contrary to what you might have read, my tween years were pretty sedate, except for being on a Nickelodeon show and having a pop star for a sister. Whenever I got home to Kentwood, I jumped right back into being just like everyone else. I enjoyed playing sports, attending church groups, and I retained my tomboy spirit. Weekends were typically spent with friends and having sleepovers at my house whenever possible. My friends and I usually got ourselves into some sort of mischief. One time I managed to almost burn down the house when my friend Crystal and I were playing with a new video camera. We decided to record one of our skits in the bathroom, where my sister had a candle burning. We became so engrossed in what we were doing and the excitement of watching ourselves that we didn't notice we'd knocked over the candle. Minutes later, our laughter was interrupted when I heard someone yelling, "What's that smell? Something is burning upstairs!" Crystal and I stared at each other in disbelief. Within minutes the flames were snuffed out and there wasn't much damage.

My family will tell you I was a precocious child. I was outspoken and mature in some aspects of my life. Although I was sassy, I rarely felt comfortable sharing my anxieties and sadness about the shifting dynamics of my family. There were two versions of me: my public persona and my true self. I was exposed to so many things during my childhood, but when it came to boys, I was innocent and genuinely naive. I never played spin the bottle or seven minutes in heaven. When I was twelve, slow dances with boys were about as naughty as I got. My partner and I would stand one foot apart with our hands placed gently just so. We'd sway slowly and do anything we could not to make eye contact. By thirteen, I was allowed to go with girlfriends to a boy's house. I remember the first time a boy held my hand throughout an entire movie, and I thought that was a big deal. My first kiss didn't happen until a couple of years later, when at fourteen, I dated a boy named Jarett Forman who was a year older than me. He was such a good guy, and the experience was sweet.

Being home also presented a set of challenges for me. My family life was never stable. My parents divorced when I was ten, but for years before that, life in the Spears house was decidedly dysfunctional. My dad's long-standing habit of disappearing for weeks at a time continued despite the angst it caused, and my momma enabled his behaviors. I was traumatized by the fallout of his alcohol abuse and developed anticipatory anxiety at the thought of him showing up drunk to any of my sporting events or performances. I feared the potential humiliation and shame that would result from him making a scene. My momma's permissiveness created tension in our relationship and made things difficult for us. I couldn't make sense of how she could divorce him because of his irresponsible and neglectful habits and then rely on him to make sensible decisions about me and my siblings. It just felt wrong.

Much of the time I spent in Louisiana, my parents were traveling for work or to assist Britney. My dad was working, and Momma was on the road with my sister for weeks at a time. She always wanted me to go on tour, but I craved the normalcy of being home. I had already spent many of my formative years on my sister's tour bus and didn't want to spend my hiatuses on one now. All I wanted was the stability of family dinners and the routine of a simple life. But that wasn't my experience. My brother, Bryan, had moved to New York, and when my parents were gone, I stayed with my friends and their families for long stretches of time. No one ever made me feel unwelcome, but the longer I stayed, the more uncomfortable I became. I always felt like I was imposing. The longing I had to be home intensified as each day passed. My active schedule helped to keep that sadness at bay. I went to school, ate lunch with my friends, and studied. I participated in activities and sports and tried to ignore the ache to be home in my own house. It became a routine: In spring and summer, I had a place and a routine. Come fall, I often found myself living a nomadic existence.

My time on *All That* gave me the confidence to start to consider moving on to something more serious. After three seasons on the show I had become a fan favorite, and with rave reviews about my performance and comedic timing. Nickelodeon approached me about developing a show where I would be the lead character. In addition to his work on *All That*, Dan Schneider wanted to develop a show around me. After talks and several brainstorming meetings together, *Zoey 101* was created. Dan thought I would be the perfect Zoey. The premise of the show was following the antics of a young teen girl and her band of friends who attended a boarding school that had just opened to girls. I was excited. Although I loved the camaraderie and daring nature of *All That*, the opportunity to act in a leading role had me ready to sign. I thought, *Wow, my own show! How awesome.* Almost immediately I started to think about how I wanted to portray this character. Who would Zoey be? How much of me might be incorporated into Zoey? I was hoping by infusing Zoey with some of my personality, she would become someone girls could relate to—a tomboy and goofy like me, yet courageous in the face of boys and bullies. I met with the show's development team and producers a few times to discuss Zoey. We had lunches where we would talk about specifics about the character and the setting for the show. The vision of Zoey became well defined, and seeing a bit of myself in her made bringing her to life seamless.

As part of the promotional campaign for *Zoey*, Nickelodeon arranged for a camera to shoot footage of me and my friend watching the premiere in a New York City hotel. After that, I never watched the show with anyone, and I never watched it by myself either. The promotion for *Zoey* was completely different from that of *All That*. The ensemble of *All That* worked as a unit or in pairs for promotional commercials and spots. As the lead in a new sitcom, I was the star with my own publicist and stylist—in a position to speak to the media and present myself to the world. In a way, I was launching myself into the next level. I was both nervous and excited to speak for myself and discuss different topics that mattered to me. I realized I had a voice and cared about how I'd be heard. I had watched my sister and other contemporaries appear on *The Ellen DeGeneres Show*, *Live! with Regis and Kelly*, *TRL*, and *Good Morning America*, and now I was on them too. I felt like I had made it. *Zoey 101* aired on January 9, 2005, and within weeks it was a hit. When it was time to return to the studio to shoot the second season of *Zoey 101*, the cast and I showed up invigorated by our success. I loved the familiarity of the set and the pace of shooting the series. The show attracted some of the best professionals in the business. The creator and director, Dan Schneider, was exacting and insisted on professionalism. He knew how to get just what he needed from a rambunctious group of teens who thought that they were all that. Scheduling and getting scenes shot in a timely fashion wasn't always so easy. Unlike *All That* I was on-screen for much of each episode. The entire crew understood that time was a factor in every shot. In the industry, working with teens and children was different from working with adults. Because of union rules, I was only permitted to work about ten hours a day. Sometimes shoots would run longer, and producers would have to come up with a way to get the scenes done. One time we were shooting an episode where I was actually in every scene. We knew we were going to run out of time. As part of the script, a bucket was placed on my head so all the scenes could be shot. A double could do the bucket scenes and I could finish out others.

Unfortunately, the camaraderie of the show's stars didn't always transfer into real life. In the first season of *Zoey 101*, Kristin Herrera, Alexa Nikolas, and I became fast friends. Kristin, who played Dana Cruz, and I clicked immediately, but all three of us spent time together on and off the set. On the weekends we would have sleepovers, go to the beach, the mall, or just hang out. We were typical girls talking fashion and boys. Alexa, who played Nicole Bristow, noticed that Kristin and I were growing closer, which caused some issues. Three is the worst number for girls because invariably one always feels left out. Throughout the shooting season we had our fair share of fun and fights, just like all girls our age. But slowly I started to feel like there was something amiss. Late into season one, rumors about me began to spread among the cast and extras. At first, it was small lies—things like people saying I was mean or bitchy. Everyone was telling me that Alexa was the one making the false claims. I went to the producers to share my concerns. Then the rumors took on a more sinister feel. I got a feeling that a few people on the set were trying to stir the pot and perhaps cause trouble between me and Alexa. I was led to believe that Alexa told extras that I smelled bad and other things that I couldn't control. I would leave the set humiliated and sad. I cried many times after work and had to hide my feelings. The way her mother walked around on set as if she owned it and whispered to her daughter incessantly—seemingly about me—raised concerns. For all I know, someone was feeding her lies that instigated the problems we experienced. I began to suspect that she was interested in having me thrown off the show in the hopes they would make Alexa the star. I did all I could to manage the situation, but over time it became more difficult. I went to the producers several times to issue complaints. After the first season Kristin left the show because the producers wanted a change, and she was replaced by Victoria Justice. The cast realized changes could be made at any time, and I wasn't experiencing any whispers or unpleasant looks. Things improved temporarily. Alexa's attention was diverted by the arrival of a new cast member, but weeks into shooting, another particularly vicious rumor spread that I had lice. Some of the extras seemed put off, and I felt an unwarranted shame.

The situation made me an emotional wreck and in need of support, so I went to my big sister for guidance.

A few days later, a very pregnant Britney came to the set to visit and have a chat with Alexa. Britney asked a PA to bring Alexa to my trailer. I was on set at the time. Alexa, who was really into fame and connections, was excited that my sister wanted to "speak" with her. The door was open when Alexa walked in. Britney didn't waste any time getting to the point. "Are you making fun of my sister? Telling lies and spreading rumors? You shouldn't do that!" Britney told her that she wouldn't keep jobs if she continued to treat people that way. Alexa scurried away from the trailer. After that chat Alexa didn't blatantly bully me, and once season two was in the can, she was dismissed from the show. She later spoke of being bullied on the set of *Zoey*.

For years I took the high road and ignored the story. I don't remember ever bullying anyone, especially a coworker on set. Considering the cruel way I felt that she treated me and tried to turn the cast and crew against me, her claims seemed designed to garner attention once her fame had waned. I can't control how she perceived our dynamic, but I can say I wouldn't have hurt her on purpose. That's just not me. Based upon everything that went on, and being thirteen, we both felt justified in our actions. Looking back, I think that all of these are normal childhood challenges. But in a working environment, with parents and producers involved, the drama of these events intensified. Some of it was a result of just too much time spent in each other's company.

I adored all the boys on the show and many others in the cast. The boys were much easier to be around at that time for me. Chris Massey, who played Michael Barret on the show, was a good friend and we still keep in touch. Sean Flynn, Matt Underwood, and Austin Butler were so much fun to be around. Erin Sanders was so much like her character, Quinn Pensky, which made it easy to like her. Sometimes it felt like the entire cast had a connection that didn't include me. Perhaps it was my own insecurity, but I think that they built stronger bonds in California while I was home most of the year in Louisiana. I was good one-on-one. But when the entire group was together, I felt a little on the friendship fringe. Oddly enough, I was a little uptight and shy at that time.

When I wasn't shooting, I spent hours in the school trailer with our teacher, Ms. Patty, and my castmates. School on set can be rigorous at times. We had to get things done in a more efficient way than regular school. Our classes were subject to time limits, and it's amazing how much you can get done in a short period. We were required to study and get things done in a way that worked with being on one of the highest rated television shows at the time. Some of my favorite memories are of the cast just being kids, goofing off and being silly. We all understood that education was a requirement, but like all kids, sometimes we had to blow off steam. We would play tricks and pranks on each other with whatever was available in the room. There were times we'd do impressions and have entertaining discussions that took us way off topic. My favorite memory is when we'd make bread as a class—like some Hollywood set home-ec class. But Ms. Patty was the absolute best and managed to get us to meet our prerequisites. We were our own weird, wonderful kind of family. Ms. Patty, who I selected to be my teacher, was more than an educator. She also served as a liaison between me and the producers. She was also responsible for protecting us and ensuring we were not overworked. Ms. Patty enforced the set laws for closing in and out, school hours, and rest. If there was a problem she would serve as a buffer or handle issues that children would have difficulty discussing. Ms. Patty stepped in when it wasn't a parent's place but the actor needed a voice. She was so patient and kind. Summer shoots were much easier and didn't require the demands of school, but we still needed Ms. Patty for all the other things she did for us. She always had our backs.

The first two seasons of *Zoey* were shot at Pepperdine University in Malibu during the school's summer break. Going into the third season, Nickelodeon moved the set to Valencia because we were going to shoot twenty-six episodes instead of the regular thirteen, which would overlap with the start of Pepperdine's school year. It took a little time to adjust to our new environment. The beach view from the coast was replaced by the abandoned warehouses of an old military base. Nickelodeon brought in a team of engineers that completely converted old buildings and parking lots to replicate our Pepperdine home. They re-created our dorm rooms and even made our lounge area in a way that made it easier to shoot scenes. For the first time we had other staging areas that also made filming simpler. When I walked on set and saw the intricate details they had copied, I was in awe. Previously we shot with one camera on-site. Now, we were on a stage.

Momma and I rented an apartment that was exactly five minutes from the set. A typical day started with me rolling out of bed, taking care of necessities, and getting to set. My days usually began early, in Mr. Michael's makeup chair. He had a morning ritual for my skin that kept it healthy. Once he was done, one of the hair people gave me my Zoey look. Then I was off to Ms. Khris in wardrobe. I loved Ms. Khris for her understanding and vision. We'd spend time discussing the episodes and the looks that worked for Zoey and me for the week of shoots.

As required by law, a parent or guardian had to be on set with us at all times, except for short periods of time when they could sign out for about ninety minutes. I was expected to act adultlike yet be treated like a child. Sometimes it was difficult to have so many people around all the time telling me what to do.

As Zoey matured, so did I. Playing the role of Zoey didn't require me to become someone completely different from myself. We were both strong-willed girls who were comfortable with their place in life. However, Zoey didn't have my real-life challenges that stemmed from the burden of so much responsibility, homesickness, and the ongoing chaos in my family. The struggles were expanding beyond just that of my parents. Bryan was trying to find his place in the world, and Britney was showing signs of a debilitating exhaustion. Bryan had difficulty holding a job, and Britney was changing right in front of my eyes. Britney had behaviors that would emerge for weeks at a time followed by periods of normalcy. Momma and Daddy would reiterate she was fine and just Britney being Britney. But the nurturing and loving mother figure I cherished—the sweet and adoring sister I admired—was changing into someone I didn't recognize. I had to hold it all together while my family desperately tried to help Britney. I was still too young to comprehend many of the issues that affected my family. We were all experiencing profound transitions in our respective lives.

I was very confused by everything and felt the only thing I could do was focus on my work and be the best professional possible. I felt the pressure of being the lead character in a TV show, managing far from home, and remaining unrelentingly professional. I was hard on myself, ensuring my weight remained low and not making any changes to my appearance. None of that seemed outrageous to me since I was portraying a character who needed to appear unchanged. But while Zoey was preserved on-screen, I was changing in real time. I went from tween to teen and went through all the changes that came with it. At times it was difficult to be the fun-loving Zoey when I was having a difficult day. I experienced the mood swings and body fluctuations that all teen girls have. I often struggled on shoot days when I was bloated from my impending period. I'd work with Ms. Khris to pick out outfits that wouldn't show the difference from one scene to the next. I believed that I appeared five pounds heavier just days before my period and remarkably lost the weight within hours of my flow starting. Ms. Khris and the wardrobe staff were kind, and I appreciated their support. Mr. Michael ended up being so much more than my makeup artist. He was like a guardian angel. My teenage skin was prone to breakouts, and he taught me the importance of good skin care. He used hot towels scented with mint and eucalyptus to cleanse my face and help me relax after a long day. He made me feel good about myself by validating how I felt. Mr. Michael was talented and worked his magic making me look fresh-faced and zit-free. But most importantly, he recognized when I was having a tough time. He would move at half speed to slow down my morning to allow me the time I needed to get my head right. Mr. Michael would take the blame if that caused a delay in the schedule.

For the span of the series, Momma and I lived in various apartments around the LA area. We moved from Santa Monica to a place in Marina del Rey and ultimately to Valencia, to be close to the show's new location. We considered moving in with my sister in Malibu, hoping to create a more cohesive family environment and support Britney, who was having a difficult time. As much as we wanted to all be together, it became increasingly obvious that something was out of whack in Britney's world. At first, I just assumed it was the fallout from her divorce and the media obsession with her. But my normally sweet and free-spirited sister continued to morph into someone else—who was disturbed and paranoid at times. Sometimes she would lash out for no apparent reason or ignore me. Invariably, Britney would feel bad and later apologize. As far as I could tell, she lacked any kind of structure or schedule to her chaotic life. Momma sensed Britney needed help, but she kept insisting she was fine.

Momma was torn between providing a safe place for me and staying close to Britney during this tumultuous period. Ultimately, we made the only sensible choice, moved into an apartment near the set, and gave our apartment a homey feel. Momma tended to my sister as much as she could. I got another dog from someone on our set. Dogs gave me unconditional love and attention that provided comfort and a reminder of home. Ally was a Yorkie poo and was by far the worst-behaved dog I ever had. She was a terror, running away and creating havoc. With my hectic schedule, I didn't have the time to give Ally the training and attention she needed. Eventually I had to give her away, too.

The typical mother–teen daughter challenges plagued Momma and me. We would lash out at each other, and I pushed her buttons when I was particularly frustrated. It all came to a head one day when she was emotionally strained and she snapped. She was angry and yelling at me, but when that didn't yield the desired effect, she started hitting me with a large beaded purse that had, among other things, a camera inside. She repeatedly swung the bag and landed several blows on my shoulders before she stopped. I left the apartment and ran to the shopping center next door to where we lived. I used a pay phone to call my brother. "Bryan, Momma's going crazy. She wouldn't let me call you or Britney."

I showed up to the set the next day to shoot the Halloween episode where I would dress up like Marilyn Monroe. While applying my makeup, Mr. Michael noticed some scratches on my neck and shoulder area. He looked at me with concern in his eyes. He asked, "What happened here, Jamie Lynn?" I shook my head and started to cry. We didn't speak, but he gave me the time I needed to deal with my emotions. Eventually, I forced all my feelings down and went to work, just like I was expected to.

I was missing home more than ever. My friends and my boyfriend, Casper, were back home in Louisiana having experiences I felt like I was missing out on. And I especially missed Casper. I met him a year and a half earlier at a church youth group event. Who could say no to a cute boy in a Dodge truck with a hog in the back? Yes, an actual large pig. At the time, he was different from the boys I knew, and he came from a rival school. He was simply an attractive boy, and I was infatuated with him. I adored having him all to myself. We started innocently with texting and talking. That's all it was for a while. Momma never let me out late or knowingly let me spend time alone with any boy. But teens always find a way. From the very beginning, Casper was slick. He coaxed me a little at a time into feeling comfortable with the physical part of our relationship. I had limited knowledge of sex and all that came with it, including birth control. I thought the rhythm method was a band from the seventies. I just let him take care of it. Sometimes he'd pick me up in town and drive until we could park to be alone. Other times we went to his house when he knew no one else would be there. Sneaking around made it more exciting. Our feelings for each other intensified.

With the distance came the idealization of him and our relationship. Our honeymoon phase was spent apart, and I was free to relive our time together and dream of more romantic days ahead. I was falling in love for the first time and didn't know how to manage being almost nineteen hundred miles apart. Sometimes I was pouty and resentful. Life was demanding for me, but less so for Momma. Bryan had relocated to California with his wife and daughter, and Britney was already a momma with her own boys, who were just one year apart. Momma had all of her kids and grandchildren in California, with plenty of time to enjoy them. She even had Daddy around when she needed him. At this point, Daddy and I weren't speaking at all. I didn't want him anywhere near us, and the times Momma would allow him in the apartment felt like a betrayal. If I was home, I locked myself in my room whenever he came over. She knew how I felt, and as a result, my resentment grew. As the dynamics between my teenage self and Momma changed, it became difficult to maintain our genial relationship. Momma walked a delicate line trying to please everyone. She failed to realize that no one can be all things to all people. Someone always gets sacrificed. Momma would take off whenever there was a supposed crisis in Malibu.

Even when things were going wrong, Momma always wanted everyone to think everything was right as rain. Appearances were paramount—not just the professional ones you showed up for. She was a great pretender, but no matter how convincing she thought she was, everyone saw through the cracks, especially me. A traitorous and powerful resentment brewed inside of me.

After long hours of shooting and school, I was expected to take care of my chores at home. My teenage brain hated her for this. She wasn't working. How come I had to take care of everything when I was the one who had a full-time job? Plagued by exhaustion, I ignored my responsibilities and refused to pick up after myself or clean. There were dirty clothes all over the floor, and even the clean ones were rarely in drawers. Occasionally, I neglected to walk my dog Ally and she made a mess inside. My room became a pigsty. I was a stressed-out teen who spent ten to twelve hours a day on set. Most days I regarded my work as a hard-earned gift. But at times I became more incensed and antagonistic. For the most part I was professional on the set, except for a handful of times when I was curt or distracted. Regardless, I always came to the set prepared. I would show up on time and know my lines. I stored up my angst for after working hours. Fortunately, I wasn't the only moody teenager on set.

Aside from the teenage angst, we had shoots that were challenging on their own merits. On one shoot, we were in the roasting California sun known for shriveling grapes into raisins. The temperature went way into the hundreds, and we were shooting on a blacktop parking lot. There were tents and portable air conditioners set up, but it didn't help the crew and extras running around.

People started to faint, and ammonia rags were kept on set to revive people. But even on those bad days, we all shared an immense sense of pride simply by being a part of the show.

I spent the better part of my early teens on *Zoey*, and my contract was coming to an end. After four seasons, Zoey had matured to a point where ending the show felt right to me, and at that point, I honestly felt like I had outgrown her. Nickelodeon and I never had a discussion about continuing *Zoey* in any form. I was ready to move on to new projects that offered me a chance to mature as an actor. Nickelodeon agreed. *Zoey 101* provided me an invaluable education on what I needed to be good at to make a show work as well as all the factors that go into a successful show. It still astounds me how all the elements have to come together—production, crew, hair and makeup, and filming, under such strict time constraints. Everyone had to work in synchronicity.

As performers, receiving accolades and awards for our work was not only validating, but it almost guaranteed we would find new jobs. As we shot the final episodes of *Zoey 101*, everyone was full of mixed emotions. We had spent years of our lives together, and we were proud of the work that made *Zoey 101* one of Nickelodeon's most highly rated shows. With the many awards and the show's notoriety, we all believed we would be able to find new opportunities. The excitement was palpable. But there was a sadness attached to the end of the show, that even we as teenagers understood. The continuity of the work had provided stability and income to everyone; the camaraderie made the days pleasurable. The show's success had executives champing at the bit. Not just one network, but other studios, production companies, and music labels reached out to me. But I didn't want to just jump into anything. I was thoughtful about what would come next.

Throughout the *Zoey* experience, I had met with music producers and other production executives, but never felt like they were interested in my professional aspirations. They recognized I was a bankable commodity as long as I was willing to be shaped and molded to their liking. Executives weren't interested in me; they were interested in the brand of Jamie Lynn Spears. They wanted to make me into something they could manipulate and sell. The past several years had locked me into playing the same character. Acting was my passion. For the first time in my career, I was going to have the freedom to choose a role or project that spoke to me on a deeper level. The prospect of employing my free will felt liberating. My plan included a move to movies and music, while others from the cast planned to continue in television. Victoria Justice was going to be the star of her own show, *Victorious*. Everyone else associated with *Zoey 101* also planned to move on to new projects in the industry.

Fans fell in love with Zoey, and now, over ten years later, fervent interest in Zoey still exists. Besides my contemporaries, who often rave to me about *Zoey 101*, there are legions of new *Zoey 101* fans who discover the reruns on Nickelodeon or online. I love that multiple generations of families have enjoyed the series. Oddly enough, my older daughter, Maddie, has very little interest in seeing me on-screen, and my younger daughter, Ivey, is too young to watch it. Whether in person or on social media, I am constantly asked about a *Zoey 101* reunion or a reboot of the show. Zoey connected with fans in such a powerful way that it's as if they have to know how she turns out as an adult. I am actively working to bring Zoey back to the screen.

The show also gave me the opportunity to sing its theme song, "Follow Me," which was cowritten by my sister. I recently produced and recorded a modern version of the song. In an effort to assuage the fans, I asked many of my original castmates to shoot a video for the song's reboot. It was tricky because we did a one-day shoot complicated by the protocols of COVID-19. The shooting schedule for that day was insane, with temperature checks and sanitation requirements. Once we all got back into a room together, the years apart vanished. We arrived as adults but performing brought us back to 2004. The release of the song and video spurred new rumors about a *Zoey 101* reunion show. I am excited at the prospect of working on another *Zoey 101* project, whether that be a long-format movie or series. The cast is eager to reunite and bring the characters into the present. We have been in talks to reinvent the series. Producers and writers have shared some concepts that sound intriguing. Hopefully, a modern-day version will go into production soon.

CHAPTER 4

Never in the Shadows

One of the greatest aspects of growing up as the youngest Spears child was having the warmth and attention of everyone in my family. From the moment I was born into the Spears family, both of my siblings made certain I was included, nurtured, and adored. Not at any point in my life did I feel like I was in competition with either of them. Britney always put me front and center—giving me the light.

Being the baby by more than nine years made my position in the family unique. My brother was a teenager when I arrived, and

Britney was already pursuing her career. Momma was working at the school, and Daddy had all kinds of jobs. When they weren't working, each one was dedicated to Bryan's and Britney's pursuits. Momma supported Britney by arranging what lessons they could afford, driving her to auditions and shows, and getting her in front of a crowd. Daddy's approach to his children's interests was completely different. As the son of an abusive perfectionist, Daddy absorbed some of the rigorous tendencies that befall children with that type of upbringing. Daddy was never physically abusive, but his unrelenting perfectionism became ingrained in each of us. By the time I cognitively understood the family credo, it had already been infused in the very synapses of my brain. If you are going to do anything, you are going to be the best at it. We weren't allowed to half-ass anything. For Bryan, that was a difficult level to achieve. He was a solid athlete and moderate student. But his performance wasn't up to Daddy's standards, and Bryan struggled with disappointing Daddy at various times. I only knew Bryan was my big brother and I adored him. Even with the age difference, he always took an interest in me. As the older brother, he would look after me and rejoice in my milestones. He never seemed annoyed by having me around and actually was amused by my precocious nature. If I sassed, he sassed me right back. He would take me out, usually with one of his girlfriends—and Bryan always had girlfriends. When I started to string sentences together, everything changed. He learned quickly that I was the boss.

One time, Momma and Daddy decided to take a night away.

Momma found it difficult to trust Bryan on his own, but his friend Jennifer was set to stay with us for the night. Britney was staying with our cousin Laura Lynn. It didn't take very long for chaos to ensue. By nightfall, I was in my room trying to sleep, and he had a backyard full of teammates and girls. I could hear everything. Someone opened my door, and I could swear he had facial hair. The noise continued and I decided to see what was going on. Kids were drinking and playing music. None of that bothered me until I saw my kiddie pool loaded with beer cans. That really made me angry. I walked over to Bryan and yelled, "Oh mister, you're in real trouble. I'm gonna tell Momma all about this." He turned me around and told me to go back to bed. The following morning, my sister came through the door, saying she heard something was going on. Bryan put Britney to work on clean-up patrol. Momma called to check in. Immediately she sensed something was wrong because Britney was being evasive. I demanded the phone and said, "Momma, Bryan had a bunch of friends here. I slept with a man with a beard and there was beer in my pool!"

The sisterly bond I share with Britney was fostered by her devotion to me as a child. Being the baby sister of Britney Spears is nothing like what people assume. From the day I arrived, I became Britney's. Momma was often working and taking care of the family. She was also dealing with the complexities of an addict husband. Britney became like a second mother to me. She was considerably older than I was, and she adored having the role of caregiver. Momma was wonderful, but my sister treated me like I was her very own American Girl doll. When I was a baby, she spent hours playing with me. She would dress me up and make sure I looked precious. At first, Momma would do my hair, but then she realized that Britney was so much better at it. Britney would wake up early to attend to me before she went to school. Our relationship grew as we did. Britney saw how theatrical I was and encouraged my early antics, which is why I developed the confidence to perform in front of others. And I was a handful. Britney would perform at regional events, and I would stand onstage and actually bow as she finished singing. My sister thought that was adorable. I cringe when I think back on some of the things I did.

When I was a toddler, Momma was forced to bring me along when my sister became part of the *Mickey Mouse Club*. That group of performers was so much fun to be around. I was everyone's little sister and drove them all crazy with my antics. One time we were enjoying the afternoon on the grounds of the place we were staying at. Suddenly, I hid from Momma, and all of the Mouseketeers were scurrying around looking for me. Little did they know, I just kept moving around a single tree trunk to remain out of view. There was a large body of water that surrounded the hotel. Momma was sobbing, worried I had fallen in the lake. The kids laughed when they found me. I just giggled and said, "Gotcha!" Britney didn't chastise me. She hugged me and whispered, "You little devil." Another time, Momma was driving a few of us from the set, and JC Chasez's dad walked up to Momma's window and spoke with her. My precocious mind took over. I leaned past Momma out the window and said,

"I already have a daddy!" Everyone laughed and I don't think anything like that ever happened again. The experience of being on the *Mickey Mouse Club* set with those amazing child performers helped me understand early on that actors, even really famous ones, were just people. We really were like a big family and to this day I think of them fondly. The cast included Christina Aguilera, JC Chasez, Ryan Gosling, Keri Russell, and Justin Timberlake, who became my sister's boyfriend on and off for many years.

Plain and simple, I adored Justin. He wasn't just my sister's boyfriend. Justin was my first example of a kind and generous young man. He and my sister were happy together for a long time. Momma and I used to go over to Justin's family's house and hang out. We swam and had cookouts. Justin was always so sweet to me, and his relationship with Britney was the only one in my life that gave me a sense of stability. That may sound strange considering how it ended, but from my perspective, they adored each other and made me a part of their relationship in the best of ways. Justin treated me like a little sister and doted on me any chance he got. I have so many memories of Britney, Justin, and me being together—many of them on car rides to one place or another. I was never a burden to either of them. One Christmas, he bought me a video camera. My sister will probably balk at my recollection, but I know that gift was all Justin. He knew I loved to create skits and thought the camera would be another creative outlet for me. I appreciated Britney's willingness to make me the third wheel in her relationship and I am eternally grateful for the memories they gave me.

Unfortunately, I was deeply affected by their split. The constancy of their relationship provided the best example of a loving couple I had ever seen. I was completely heartbroken when it was over and believed that it was a devastating loss in Britney's life as well.

I watched as my sister became pop star Britney Spears, and then the one-named icon, Britney. Life for her changed daily, but oddly enough, for many years, not much changed in terms of her role in my life. She doted on me as an infant and continued to do so as I began to sing and create my own skits. My sister showered me with attention, love, and praise well into my teens. Like Momma, she was one of my biggest cheerleaders and told me that I was talented and going to be an amazing performer. To show her support, my sister continued to make me the nightly star on the tour bus and gave me the platform to perform for the crew. I spent months on her various tours and those experiences actually helped build my confidence. My skits are legendary—well, at least to those who spent time on the tour buses. But my sister was more than my cheerleader.

Britney became cross with me just a handful of times. She had created a small child-sized playhouse in our backyard. The playhouse was a replica of a house with a kitchen and living area. As a kid, I was running wild—collecting frogs and insects. I started to collect my specimens, put them in the playhouse, and create my own animal farm. By the time Britney returned from a summer stint in New York, I had just about destroyed her playhouse. She wasn't so happy with me then and used some choice words to tell me so. But Britney, who was prone to hold grudges with others, forgave me within days.

Beyond the support and adoration, Britney was simply a terrific sister. That's not just me paying homage to a living legend. For many years, she was good at keeping her persona out of our sisterhood. The rest of it—the stardom, talent, and turbulent media shitstorm—that's got very little to do with the sister I love. The only reason I mention the gossip that's been reported in the tabloids is to say that so much of what has been written about her is a diluted version of the truth. I'm not here to debunk the falsehoods written about my family; I only want to confess my experiences and the complicated blessings of being part of the Spears family. Long before articles and reports about Britney dominated news outlets, the paparazzi were infringing on her personal space and private life. I watched her suffer the bullish and offensive verbal attacks and the way photographers would hound her whenever she was in public. Frankly, there were many times the paparazzi would violate private moments as well. One such instance, when Momma and Britney took me and a friend to the local pet store, ended disastrously. By the time we were ready to leave the shop, a mob of people and photographers surrounded the storefront and our car. I was huddled in the back seat with my friend in disbelief. As Momma tried to move the car forward slowly, she and Britney were yelling in vain to get people to move out of the way. A man started screaming that she had run over his foot. Momma was shouting that it wasn't true. He told his wife to call 911. Once the police arrived, Momma insisted that the man was lying and demanded that an officer go with the couple to the hospital to make sure he didn't try to inflict damage on himself. She was worried he'd hit himself with a hammer or something. It was complete pandemonium. As it turned out, the man was evaluated by the local hospital and hadn't suffered any injuries. But this kind of reaction was a regular occurrence anytime my sister tried to go out in public. I wasn't quite a household name yet, but if we went anywhere together, cameras and lights went off at fantastical speeds.

Some people feel the paparazzi have the right to photograph a public figure no matter the circumstances. But what most people don't truly understand is that fame doesn't dehumanize you—it actually forces you to respect and appreciate your privacy. With the help of California lawmakers, and after multiple dramatic incidents, politicians realized legislation needed to be enacted to protect people from the paparazzi. In 2009, a law was passed that is sometimes referred to as "the Britney Law." I was happy when I learned there would be protections in place for both famous and private citizens.

As I mentioned, the recorded skit sessions on my sister's tour bus are what led to me catching the eye of a Nickelodeon producer. Britney believed I could accomplish anything, and she made sure to tell me and everyone else. It never occurred to me I could possibly fail. That didn't even register in my head. I was privy to watching and sharing in my sister's journey to success, and honestly, I thought, *If she can do it, so can I.* Momma made us believe that anything was possible if we dedicated ourselves to it; Daddy taught us that if you are going to do it, you must be the best. With those tenets reinforced year after year, and watching Britney's rise to fame, how could I feel any other way? It was never if, but *how* was I going to get there?

From the minute Nickelodeon showed an interest, my road to achieving my dreams was paved. There is no denying that Britney's fame opened doors for me. But once inside, I had to prove I had talent and a strong work ethic. Studios hire actors all the time and keep the ones who continue to perform. I had to prove myself every day. I wasn't handed anything. My sister was so excited for me when she learned I was hired for *All That*. She understood that a children's variety show could lead to bigger things. Although Britney was in the midst of an explosive career, she always made time for me and supported my show by making periodic appearances. I loved having her on set and her visits gave us a chance to catch up. It didn't hurt the ratings either.

As I mentioned earlier, Momma and I were living in the house off Sunset Boulevard where Britney and Justin lived. I was filming just a few miles away and they were off performing much of the time. When she wasn't touring and I had a few hours off, we would hang out as sisters. Despite our age gap, our life experiences brought us closer. We would spend the days in the pool, making up dances and acting out impromptu performances. One time my sister choreographed a routine to P!nk's song "Get the Party Started" for me. We used my video camera and Britney directed the whole thing.

After hours perfecting the moves, she filmed me in our homemade elaborate video. I was singing to the camera, being my sassy self, and feeling like I was a star. It was typical of my sister to make me feel cool. There were times we spent all afternoon surveying her property. Britney had lemon trees that I swear grew more than just lemons. In reality, there were probably a couple of different fruit trees planted amongst the lemons. We'd pick fruits and run around on the hills. I was still a kid and Britney was a kid at heart. When we were in Louisiana we spent our days building forts. She would take me and my friends into town and we loaded up the car with gear, like wood, tape, and tarps. We spent hours creating our private world and enjoying the outdoors, and it gave all of us a chance to be kids. I think being with me, just playing, allowed Britney to return to a part of her life she missed.

My early years in Hollywood were made better by having my sister be an integral part of the experience. But by the time I was twelve and learning about the darker side of fame, my sister's struggles in her own life and the media had intensified.

In December 2003, my family spent Christmas in Kentwood. My sister surprised Momma with a new Mercedes. On Christmas Eve, Britney and Bryan took the car and went out partying. Britney was looking to party away the pain of her breakup with Justin. They caught up with Jason Alexander, an old friend from town. Jason and Britney grew up together but went to separate schools. The story goes that as a toddler in daycare, Jason was bullying a classmate. Four-year-old Britney intervened and beat him up. Jason grew into a hotshot in our small town. He was often up to no good and everyone knew he was bad news. But Britney was not thinking about any of that. She and Bryan didn't return until the following morning, looking like they had been up all night. The car was a mess inside. All kinds of garbage, bottles, and even a razor blade littered the back seat. Horrified, Momma wanted no part of that car. But it was Christmas, and we were all going to smile.

Still, my sister's generosity knew no bounds. Britney arranged for a girls' trip to the Caribbean island of Nevis. Our aunt Sandra had been battling cancer, and we were all looking forward to the vacation. The day after Christmas, Momma, Aunt Sandra, Britney, Laura Lynn, me, and a couple of friends flew to Nevis. Immediately, I noticed Britney was being secretive and keeping her distance. She smoked a lot of cigarettes and drank cocktails. My sister, who was still like a mother to me and who was always put together, started to unravel even in the way she presented herself. It was weird for me to see her disheveled. We were getting dressed to go to dinner, and I suggested a cute dress similar to the one Laura Lynn was wearing. Britney scoffed, "You want me to dress like a grandma? Huh?" This was the first time she snapped at me in such a dismissive way. She didn't have any interest in being with her lifelong best friend, Laura Lynn, and left us to go do their own thing. She wanted to be anywhere but with us. I was particularly pained by her shunning. After years of making me a priority and spending time together, my sister was now moving on without me. I felt like I was Woody from *Toy Story*. I had been her favorite until I was replaced by her version of Buzz Lightyear. Her indifference was hard for me to process.

Britney had no intention of slowing down. The partying continued that week. We landed back at the private airport in Hammond on New Year's Eve, and as everyone but Britney and Laura Lynn exited the plane, Jason and a few of their friends got on to fly to Las Vegas for New Year's. I just knew this was a bad idea. Something was way off with her. The last thing I said before she left was, "Now don't go and marry Jason while you're there, Britney!" She rolled her eyes at me and said the equivalent of "as if." But sure enough, within hours we got word that in a haze of substance she had married him. My parents flew out to Vegas to minimize the disaster. I was left behind, forced to deal with gossip and chatter from everyone all over town. I shadowed my embarrassment and humiliation by downplaying the whole fiasco and pretending it was blown out of proportion. Inside I was scared and unsure of how to manage. I felt abandoned.

The marriage ended within hours, but the chaos of my sister's life was just beginning. Jason still tries to make himself relevant in Britney's life by talking all kinds of nonsense. He even gives the occasional interview discussing our family, trying to stir up interest in himself.

My sister returned to Louisiana, and my family managed damage control and tried to minimize the media fallout. Everyone was more concerned with the public perception than my sister's emotional state. Britney continued to act erratically, and all I wanted was her interest and approval. I wanted my sister back. But instead, I saw the depth of her difficulty. She was paranoid and erratic. One time, she said to me, "Baby, I'm scared," and took a large knife from the kitchen, pulled me along to my room, and she locked us both inside. She put the knife in the bedside table drawer and simply repeated, "I'm scared." She needed me to sleep beside her. Within days of this episode, Britney was packing up and headed back to her life in LA. I knew something was very wrong, and I was powerless to do anything about it. Everyone was too invested and didn't want to do what should have been done. Something was off, and I had a shaky feeling when she left.

Bryan's life was just as crazy, but without the fame. He was still struggling with work, and even worked for both me and Britney at times. He had other jobs along the way, too. He settled in New York for a time, and I loved going there to visit. We had a routine that would take us to our favorite spots, which included the Times Square restaurant Mars 2112 and FAO Schwarz. Bryan was a charmer, and he attracted women like bees to honey. He eventually started seeing my manager, Graciela, and they got engaged. But his struggles with employment and managing money continued.

Mostly, though, I was an egocentric tween, and I was able to compartmentalize and keep all the family drama far from my thoughts. I was wrapped up in being me—the tween television star and the Southern tomboy who loved home.

Once I signed on to do *Zoey 101*, I felt confident in the trajectory of my career. Britney was more balanced at that time, and I felt a great sense of relief that she was doing well. She had found love with Kevin Federline, gotten married, and had two beautiful boys. Her emotional fluctuations, which I called episodes, were well managed, and no one ever learned anything about her struggles. My family believed that was best for everyone. I went along with them because I was taught to support my family in all things.

I loved that Britney made her home near where I was shooting, and we could hang out whenever our schedules permitted. As fans discovered the show, my name began to appear in magazines and online reports. Photographers shot pictures of me, and I began to get a sense of what my sister's constant violation felt like. Anytime we went anywhere together, the number of paparazzi tripled. It was insane. I hated the attention and would avoid it any way possible. During my shooting schedule, there wasn't much free time to go out, and even as I got older, I didn't have the desire to go to Hollywood parties. Some part of me was affected by seeing the negative impact of so much attention on my sister, and I'd experienced some of the hostility she dealt with myself.

Despite my adoration for Britney, she was changing once again. She began to experience a particularly difficult episode. My fun-loving and sweet-natured sister lost her softness. This time I attributed her troubles to her divorce and having two babies in a single year. Again, she became distant, even when we were sitting three feet away from each other. She was moody, and her erratic behaviors were troubling. At the beginning of *Zoey*, she would make the occasional visit to hang out on set. Everyone loved having her there, especially me. By the end of the third season, when Sam Lutfi had infiltrated her life, the sister I knew was vanishing. She came to a *Zoey* shoot in a mood. The amiable Britney was gone. In her place was an agitated woman, angry enough with Momma to yell at her in public. It was the first time I was ever embarrassed by her. Both Momma and I just made excuses for her behavior for a while. Britney was being isolated from the good people in her life by Sam, a man who weaseled his way into her life with big stories and empty promises.

Months before Sam Lutfi became Britney's self-proclaimed gatekeeper, he tried to lure Momma into some jewelry scheme, hawking stones on HSN. Momma met him through Paul Butcher's mom, Jackie. Paul played Dustin, my little brother on *Zoey 101*. Momma and I went to the Grove, a shopping and dining complex in LA, to speak with Sam. From the moment I met him, I knew he was bad news. I told Momma, "He's creepy and makes my skin crawl." I didn't want him anywhere near us. She met with him a second time and rejected his proposal. For a while there was no word from him. Weeks later, my sister was at a nightclub and Sam introduced himself to her, claiming he was a friend of Momma's. We didn't know if he coordinated this introduction or just happened to be at the same club. Sam slowly insinuated himself into her life. He conned Alli Sims, a family friend who was Britney's assistant at the time. Britney was vulnerable after her divorce from Kevin Federline, and Alli was there to help with just about everything, including the kids. Alli liked to claim we were all cousins, but that's not true. Sam manipulated Alli, or maybe she was in on it with him. To this day, I can't be sure. Britney became Sam's target, and he painstakingly dismantled her life. Slowly, Britney's previous team members were disappearing, and Sam began to take charge of everything in my sister's world. To me he seemed both pathological and manipulative. He'd call the paparazzi before Britney went out. When I asked him why he did this, he'd deny it even when I saw him making the call. Later he claimed he did it to alleviate Britney's anxiety about the press. He'd make appointments with producers and deny doing it. He continued to isolate Britney from Daddy and Momma. He'd lock them out of the house and refuse them access to their grandbabies. It seemed like he was always looking at properties and trying to get Britney to rent various homes in the area. I didn't understand his role in her life. I started to ask Britney why he was there, and she said she didn't know. Finally, I took it upon myself to try and get him to leave. "Sam, why are you here? You should leave. No one needs you here!" His answer was, "Come on, Jamie Lynn. You like me." I was baffled. I yelled, "I do not like you!" Even at sixteen, I recognized he was a truly evil force in our lives.

Things got worse. I was the only family member allowed in the house. On my next visit, when I tried once again to get rid of him, he attempted to manipulate me too. "Hey, Jamie Lynn. I know your parents don't want your boyfriend to come to LA. I got a house set up that you both can stay in. I can get Casper a job where he can make all kinds of money." I stared at him in disbelief.

"I'm not doing that!" What kind of grown-up man offers that to a teenage girl?

Sam's manipulations continued, and he told her all kinds of things to justify an exclusive role in her life. I was very suspicious of the situation. I sensed that drugs were readily available at the house. Although I never saw anything, my sister's erratic behavior was enough to make me cautious. I never ate or drank anything when I visited, fearful that something was dissolved in her Gatorades and juices.

Sam became enraged if you didn't answer a question or ignored him. He was gaining influence over Britney—how she spent her time and money. With each visit I became more apprehensive. I was young, but not naive. Suspicion spiked when I noticed that her usual assistants, who coordinated appointments and were a part of her entourage, were dismissed, and replaced with some seriously questionable characters. I became very uncomfortable in the house.

It was apparent that many aspects of her life were not completely within her control. Sam was intimidating and had an obvious influence over some of the decisions she was making. Britney seemed skittish and yet looked for approval from him. He was setting up appointments with producers he had no right to, and at one point, I was forced to intercede on Britney's behalf. She was uncomfortable and wouldn't meet with a producer who showed up at her house without her knowledge. She ran upstairs and locked herself in her bedroom. Through a speakeasy door, which was a small sliding panel in her bedroom door, she begged me to get rid of the guy. Reluctantly, I did as I was asked, but I noticed that over a few weeks, her behavior became increasingly more erratic. My meager failed attempts to remove him from her life left me feeling powerless to help her.

I knew she had been through a lot in a short period, and I thought that maybe the combination of stardom, motherhood, and a public divorce was just too much to handle, rendering her vulnerable to bad influences. Her life seemed hazy, like looking through unfocused binoculars. I was sixteen and didn't understand the demons surrounding my sister; I only knew something felt off-kilter. But in reality, she was struggling to manage the fallout from Sam's scheming. This left her an emotional wreck with no one she felt she could trust.

He continued to call me and my family after he was removed from Britney's life. That just felt like a sad attempt to remain a part of our lives. When I became pregnant with Maddie, he tried to reach out but I shut that communication down immediately. To me, Sam Lutfi exemplifies an insidious culture of people who use other people to leverage themselves. They prey on the vulnerable and impaired for their own gain, using anyone susceptible to their attentions. And Britney was at her lowest when he came along. Sadly enough, Sam Lutfi continues to make outrageous claims from his time with my sister. Most recently, he tried to get Momma in on another one of his schemes. Now, she has a long-term restraining order against him.

Britney's behavior became more unstable until it all came

to a head. With the support of my parents, Britney got the help she needed. At the time, the conservatorship was enacted, and a restraining order was issued to protect Britney from Sam. I have very little doubt that Sam was primarily responsible for complicating my sister's preexisting emotional trauma.

I knew Britney had been through so much in the past few years and wanted to believe her downward spiral was temporary. Britney continued to support my efforts and be the best sister she could at that time.

The spotlights on my sister were blinding and obscured her ability to recognize the dangers all around her—dangers that still exist. Sometimes I feel like Britney's light was too bright, and I should have done more to protect her.

CHAPTER 5

Pregnancy and Perception

When the lights faded on the final episode of *Zoey 101*, I experienced so many mixed emotions. This was the end of an era and a show that changed the course of not just my life, but the lives of all of my castmates and crew. Everyone was going in different directions, and I felt like my compass was spinning. Several opportunities were available to me to continue working and expand my audience. What should I do now? More television? Movies? Finish high school and then college? Or strike while the iron was still hot and I was relevant? It was a scary and uncertain time, and yet I welcomed the chance to go home and relax again.

I felt untethered and had nothing professionally or personally to ground me. I didn't have a job, and Casper and I had recently split again. Being a young television star and maintaining a healthy relationship with a teenage boy far away was difficult to say the least. We were together for a long time, and I was lost in the powerful feelings that come with first love, or what I thought was love. The array of feelings and anxiety that coursed through me made me doubt the decision to stop seeing him.

Our relationship became more serious season after season. I got to know his family and he got to know mine. He came out to LA so we could be together, and he was even an extra on the show. But the months apart took their toll. I truly loved him but wasn't really sure how to make a relationship work when I was away so much. By the time *Zoey* ended, we were struggling to stay together. There were rumors about him spending time with other women, but he became irritated when I hung out with male friends. I started to question whether we were worth fighting for. I knew we needed to reconnect, or I had to figure out how to let him go. We were headed in different directions, and one or both of us needed to change course. After almost two years together, it became painfully obvious that the intensity of first love was waning and I broke it off.

With a gap in my schedule, I took advantage of an opportunity to get away. After we wrapped the show, Nickelodeon graciously gifted me with a trip to the Bahamas. I invited my friend Kasey to join me on the celebratory trip, and I left the world behind and avoided making decisions about my future. The Bahamian people were welcoming, and the scenery beckoned us to chill. We had a great time hanging out in the sun and enjoying the tropical vibe. Kasey and I were both very conservative, but we even managed to try the local beer, which neither of us could stomach. Once we returned to LA, we spent our time doing all of the things I'd never made time for while working. We visited the Getty Museum, went to the beach, and attended a few celebrity parties. I was never into the nightlife of LA but thought I should give it a chance. People were nice enough, but I enjoyed being a homebody.

Breaking up with Casper proved more difficult than I thought, though. It wasn't long before we resumed texting and talking again. Soon, I flew home to Louisiana and reunited with him. During that week, we spent most of our time together. Casper convinced me we could make it work. We tried to have fun and went to an LSU game. But as soon as I took my seat on the plane back to LA, I had doubts. The whispers of him stepping out on me started up again, becoming harder to ignore, and I just knew it was over. It took a little time to bolster up the courage to break it off, but I finally ended it.

My team encouraged me to immediately start the audition pro- cess. Nickelodeon was supportive of my desire to move on to new projects, and I was steeling myself for the challenges that come with change. With my previous success, the future of a long-term career in the entertainment industry was promising. I needed a little time to regroup after another breakup and wasn't quite ready to jump into my next project. I spent most of my time in the LA apartment I shared with my momma, but when I wanted space and quality time with my sister, I went to Britney's house. I'd go there all the time simply to enjoy the space and beauty of the area. The time I spent with her in Malibu allowed us to be cocooned in a secluded place and just be sisters. When it was just the two of us, we were a couple of typical girls hanging out and enjoying our sisterly bond. But outside of that, it was difficult to make sense of Britney's world, and I started to feel different about staying at her house. I became very uncomfortable there. Britney tried to reassure me that everything was fine and, as the little sister, I believed her. After a few days together, she persuaded me to get back to work. The whole scene made me uncomfortable, and I just wanted out of there.

Over the next few weeks, I woke daily feeling out of sorts. I was nauseated and all I wanted to do was sleep. Exhaustion plagued me. Days passed and my irritability spiked. Feelings of nostalgia and a profound homesickness were ever present. Team Jamie Lynn assumed I was just being a typical moody teen and pushed me to keep working. But I suspected something was wrong. I continued to work, appearing on the Ashton Kutcher TV project *Miss Guided* and reading for movie roles. But my perpetual fatigue and malaise finally got the best of me. I went in to read for a potential blockbuster movie about teen vampires. Even the premise of *Twilight* sounded completely ridiculous. Walking in, I turned to Momma and said, "This concept doesn't seem like something that people are going to buy into." But I ignored my discomfort, nibbling on crackers to soothe my roiling stomach, and waited my turn. I had a whole conversation that I can't recall because I was so plagued with queasiness, but waved to Lily Collins from across the room. Sitting in the waiting area with so many other actors, the nausea and anxious feeling finally hit a tipping point. I felt so sick that once I was called in, I couldn't give my reading the respect or enthusiasm it required. I was always one for professionalism, so my lack of effort was alarming. I needed to leave. Not just the studio. I needed to pack up and return home to Louisiana.

The decision to go home eased my tension, and I thought my persistent worry and weariness would be eliminated. Returning to a familiar and welcoming environment was just the medicine I needed. My life had changed so much in a short time. I felt the burden of being unemployed, and Casper and I were officially over. Big decisions about my future could wait. My plan was to live in my shorts and sweatshirts and hang out with friends for a while.

Once I was back in Kentwood, I returned to the simplicity of life in Momma's house—sleeping in late, catching up with friends, and attending high school instead of the tutoring I had received on set. I got up for school and made it to my classes on time, but my friend Jessica noticed I was dragging. Emotions were getting the best of me, and that queasy feeling wasn't getting any better. I was still trying to convince myself it was just the release of stress after so many months of working, the end of the show, and the breakup.

But when the nausea didn't subside, and I realized I'd missed my period, I started to think about the last time Casper and I were intimate. We hadn't been together like that in a while, so I spent days convincing myself there was no way I could be pregnant. Then I recalled the weekend in September when I flew in for an LSU game. I felt the stirrings of panic. This was when I first seriously considered the possibility I was pregnant.

At first, I was freaking out. I panicked and felt a sense of fear that I never experienced before. The fear persisted, but as the days passed, a sense of acceptance began to take root. Jessica and I spoke daily, but it took me some time before I confided in her that something wasn't quite right. We were hanging out at my house when I broached the subject and she asked me if I thought I might be pregnant. I couldn't deny the possibility. She said, "Jamie Lynn—I think you really need to take a test."

By the time I tossed on my shorts and T-shirt, I was sick with nerves. I took the keys to my mom's two-seater Lexus, not realizing I was leaving my house as a child for the last time. To this day, if you asked me what roads I took or what was on the radio, I couldn't tell you. Jessica and I drove around for a long time, trying to figure out what to do. There was no way either of us could walk into a store to buy a pregnancy test without being recognized. I didn't mean people would recognize me, the teen star; I meant it was a small town and anyone we ran into would recognize local kids Jamie Lynn and Jess. Who could I trust to help me with such a sensitive issue? We devised a plan. I knew instinctively my mom was out of the question. She would flip out. My family knew everyone, and in a small town, news traveled faster than a rocket. Just when I thought I'd hyperventilate, Jess and I thought about our friend Ms. Heidi, who was a few years older than us and lived a couple of towns over. She was young at heart and enjoyed hanging out with us. We called her and pleaded with her to go to the store, buy the test, and stick it in her mailbox. Ms. Heidi's help was a huge relief. At least I wouldn't have to risk getting caught in the store.

A little while later, we drove by and grabbed the test from her mailbox. The minute I got my hands on that test, I swear I thought I was going to puke. Between my racing heart and turbulent thoughts, it became difficult to focus on my driving. Out of desperation, we pulled into the BP gas station off Veterans Boulevard, knowing it had a single-stall bathroom, no keys, no questions, and no interruptions. Jess locked the door, and I did what girls in my situation do—sit, stick, and wait.

There's a universal truth about time. It speeds up in the good moments and crawls during times of anticipation. Those few minutes in the bathroom really felt like an eternity. I felt like I was in some weird vortex. A series of thoughts were popping like bubbles off a wand. *What if? Oh shit! What are my parents going to say? My daddy is going to kill him. What's going to happen to my career? I've always been the "good" girl. A baby? Could I be a mom? I'm going to lose everything I worked hard for. But a baby!* In an attempt to staunch the flow of thoughts, I focused on the cracks on the floor, the fluorescent lighting, and the muted voices from outside. As I sat there, so much of the past several weeks started to make sense. But at my age, how was I supposed to know what pregnancy felt like? Jessica was yelling, "He's a dirty dog, your ex–piece of shit." She'd never liked Casper, and now she was cursing him to high heaven for putting me in this situation. She was so angry on my behalf, but I had no room in my head for anger.

I was going to have an answer in a matter of minutes. The seconds ticked by, and the anticipation was making me queasier than ever. The plastic stick sat on the edge of the sink taunting me, waiting to determine my future. We stared at it from a distance in terror. Holy crap! My life could be changed forever. Tears sprang to my eyes and I couldn't look. So, like a good friend, Jessica did it for me. She picked it up. I will never forget the expression on her face as she looked from me to the positive test and back again, the shock setting in. My world stopped in an instant and I froze. All but one of the thoughts from minutes ago evaporated: How was I going to look my momma in the eyes and say the words "I'm pregnant"?

As the shock wore off, my synapses were firing, and I felt dizzy. What to do first? Who to tell? I went with the obvious choice, which was to call Casper on the phone and tell him. He didn't believe me. He thought it was a ploy.

I said, "A ploy for what?"

He insinuated I slept around and even if I was pregnant, maybe the baby wasn't his. He was the only person I had ever been intimate with. Still, Casper wasn't convinced. We hung up and I was reeling. Confused and still feeling wretched, I asked, "What do I do now?"

My inner voice kept repeating, *I'm going to have a baby*. I reached out to my good friend Diane from McComb, Mississippi, whose support and quick thinking got me the help I needed. Thankfully, just about everyone is connected in McComb. Diane made a call to a close family friend who was a doctor at the McComb OB-GYN Associates office. She explained my situation to Dr. Dawn, and we met at the clinic's back door the following morning. The sneaking around heightened my nervousness. At points I thought my heart would beat right out of my chest. The moment felt surreal, especially when Dr. Dawn gestured toward the examining room. Diane and Jessica waited in an adjacent office while the doctor examined me and performed an ultrasound, where I heard my baby's heartbeat for the first time. I was already seven weeks along, and my little "froggy" had a strong heart, with a rhythm that lived within me. That unfamiliar repetitive swooshing sound permeated every molecule of the space. I felt such awe and an overwhelming sense of peace hearing her heartbeat—as if she was saying, "Momma, Momma, Momma." Then my stomach flipped like I was in a free fall. I was going to be a mother.

It took several seconds for me to register that Dr. Dawn was speaking to me. Her tone was both professional and compassionate when she said, "Jamie Lynn, you need to call your momma ASAP. You are a minor and as such your parents need to be notified immediately." My initial reaction was pure panic, followed by hysteria. I wasn't sure I could do it. I thought of a few different ways to tell her. "Hey, Momma? Guess what? You're going to be a grandma again." Or, "You're never going to guess what happened to me!"

I got ahold of myself and picked up the phone to call her. I tried two times and thank goodness she didn't answer. The Lord had spared me for a little while. I was so relieved I teared up for the second time in two days. I sat on the exam table quietly cradling my flat stomach and contemplated the reality of the baby growing inside of me. Dr. Dawn shared more prenatal information, along with a prescription for prenatal vitamins and a sonogram of my baby. I stared at the picture for a long time. That visual image was life altering for me. My baby was real, and at that moment, I became a mom.

After several attempts to reach my ex to share the official news, we drove around, went to a McDonald's drive-through, and I bought me my very first Happy Meal. The chicken nuggets and french fries were delicious, and the time to let everything sink in was invaluable. I thought, *I'm going to be a momma!* Jessica was ranting: "Casper…ugh, he's awful…I hate him and what he's done to you…When I get my hands on him…" Diane, on the other hand, was deep in thought. Minutes later she put it all out there.

"Jamie Lynn, you know the press is going to get ahold of this story. It will either be 'Child Star Gets Knocked Up and Has an Abortion,' or 'Jamie Lynn Spears Pregnant at Sixteen, No Longer America's Good Girl.' It's media madness no matter what."

I knew that all of that was true. I was freaking out about how the world would perceive all of it. I was young, famous, unmarried, and pregnant—talk about a media shitstorm. I was basically throwing a grenade onto my well-constructed career path. *Kapow.* I placed my hand on my belly to try and focus on my baby. I knew I should care more about the fallout of the pregnancy, but right then, none of that mattered to me. I just knew I was going to have my baby and nothing and nobody was going to change that fact.

We got back into the car and drove out to Liberty, Mississippi, where Casper was living with too many freedoms because his dad was out of town for work. He answered to no one and spent his days drinking and partying. Knocking on the door was a waste of time. No one answered. I was getting frustrated and decided we would do something drastic to get Casper's attention. We bought a cheap frame to ensure the sonogram picture didn't fly away and left it perched on the front door. We drove off and then waited for the phone to ring.

By now, Momma was frantic. She was calling all over looking for me, so I had to get home and pacify her. Acting came natural to me and she was convinced everything was fine, but internally I was freaking out. Several hours later Casper finally called claiming all kinds of bullshit, saying things like, "How do I know the baby is mine? Your name isn't even on this sonogram. It's not your test." I tried to explain everything, but my words were jumbled with emotion that made it difficult to speak. It had never occurred to me that he'd question my integrity. I had never cheated. I decided to go back to his house to talk in person. I explained the time line and the facts. The doctor couldn't put my name on the ultrasound because I was a minor and hadn't been given permission to administer the test. It took a while, but he was finally convinced the baby was his.

Soon after, we told his parents, who took the news well. Then we went to my house to tell Momma. It no longer mattered that we had broken up or that I was conflicted by my emotions. We were pregnant and from the moment I saw that tiny life on the screen and heard the heartbeat, I was determined to have this baby. If I said it enough times to myself, it would happen.

He drove us to my house so we could tell my mom. Wordlessly we got out of the car and walked to the front door. We just stood there, the magnitude of the moment making it impossible to speak. Casper and I were lost in our own thoughts and feelings, but at that moment I was relieved he was there with me. We went into the house and my internal freak-out continued. The fear of telling Momma was crippling. I just couldn't speak the words.

Instead, I scribbled the words on a note, unceremoniously dropped it in front of her, and ran from the room. I hurried to the couch to sit next to Casper, in need of his support. And then, we waited. It didn't take very long.

"JAMIE LYNN! You're pregnant? Is this a joke?"

At first, Momma wasn't mad, but rather in a state of disbelief. "But we just had the talk about all of that." Her words were bittersweet. "Jamie Lynn, you're my baby, having a baby." It was obvious that worry suffused her tone. Momma reached out to Bryan first and told him that there was a problem. I think Momma was so concerned with how Daddy would react, she had Bryan call him.

The day after I told Momma about the baby, I went to school in an attempt to keep up appearances. Slowly, reality started to set in. This baby was going to disrupt my entire life. Was I prepared to sideline my career for an indefinite amount of time, unsettling the team of professionals who had helped me along the way? Would everyone lose their job? It occurred to me that this decision affected so many people. That thought got me thinking about what might happen. The ramifications of the pregnancy were far reaching. As a performer with fame, I understood the importance of confidentiality, especially in a situation like this. I knew in my heart that shit was going to hit the fan and I needed to ensure viable communication with the people I trusted. After school I drove to the Walmart to buy a couple of burner phones.

I came home from school, and Daddy and Bryan were there. A single day had elapsed before Daddy's anger brought out the sense of dread everyone felt about my situation. Once Momma and Daddy told my team, things spiraled out of control pretty quickly. When I walked in, Daddy, Bryan, and Momma were in the house and Ms. Lou Taylor, of Tri Star, my financial management team, was on the phone. There was a whole lot of fighting going on between everyone involved. The entire Spears team was already caught up in my sister's PR difficulties, and everyone around me just wanted to make this "issue" disappear. My family and management pulled me out of school until they could figure out what to do next. They took my smartphone away, fearing the news would get out, and insisted that no one share any information with anyone, especially the press. My daddy and I stopped speaking and the tension was terrible.

For the first few days, I spent most of the time in my room. Everyone had their own opinion about what was best for me. One person after another—and there were many—came to my room trying to convince me that having a baby at this point in my life was a terrible idea. There was lots of chatter, but none of it felt right to me. It will kill your career. You are just too young. You don't know what you're doing. There are pills you can take. We can help you take care of this problem. Think about what you're doing to your family. Doesn't the family have enough to deal with? I know a doctor. There are procedures that remedy mistakes like this. You don't have to do this. He's a louse. He'll never be able to care for the baby or you. Jamie Lynn, don't make a mistake you'll regret for the rest of your life. I'll never forget that last plea—of making a mistake I would regret—because it reinforced my decision to have my baby.

Discussions continued, and everyone was certain that termination would be the best course of action. I will never forget when Ms. Lou stood up for me and said, "Y'all can't force her to abort the baby." She was the first and only person on my team to show any support for my desire to keep my baby. The next option was for me to go to Mercy Ministries, a home for unwed mothers in Tennessee, where I could eventually give up my baby for adoption. Daddy and I fought, slinging words and tossing insults. He grabbed me by the shoulders and held on tightly in the hopes of bending me to his will. I got in his face and yelled, "NO! I won't go." I couldn't deal with any of them. I ran away from them, panting with rage.

Despite my decision to have my baby, I struggled with self-loathing, guilt, and panic. I was smart enough to know that I was essentially a child, having a baby. But childhood would fade quickly as Froggy grew in my belly. I knew this situation was going to derail my career, and I knew that my parents were ashamed of me. I'd spent my entire life trying to be the perfect daughter, performer, and professional. I was always under so much pressure to make everyone's life easier, including my own. I was all things to all people. Now, the pressure to maintain that image and manage the disappointment was suffocating. With all the chaos surrounding my sister, I never wanted to be a burden to my family. My family had their own version of what was right. With the pregnancy, my sense of right became the opposite of theirs. I needed help figuring out what to do. Those burner phones came in handy. I periodically changed the SIM cards for security and spoke with the few friends who supported me.

I remained sequestered, while preventing a press leak became my team's priority. Contracts were drafted and nondisclosures signed by Casper and anyone who might try to benefit from releasing the story. My team, who I realized had a difficult time supporting my decision, still managed to help me move through the myriad of business concerns. Daddy took off to California to be with my sister and Momma—well, she was there. I agreed to cut an exclusive deal with *OK!* magazine to release the pregnancy story and the first pictures of me and my baby to the world. It was the only way I felt I could have some control over the situation. Social media wasn't the platform it is today, and everyone felt that an exclusive deal would be the best way to tell my story. If this had happened to me once social media became the all-consuming medium it is today, my experience would have been different. Some of my trauma may have been avoided, but the onslaught of the world weighing in with their thoughts and opinions would have been even more damaging. Social media will always be a double-edged sword; it can defend and inform, just like it can damage and destroy.

At that time, the deal had very little to do with money, and everything to do with limiting the potential media storm. My team arranged for someone to walk me through the process, but in the end the pregnancy article became a blend of coached answers and my own true feelings.

Home felt like a prison without a smartphone or connection to the outside world. My team believed everyone outside of the inner circle was a potential threat. They went so far as hiding my pregnancy from my sister, claiming, "It's too risky to tell Britney about the baby." I needed her more than ever, and she wasn't able to help me in my most vulnerable time. Britney's condition was spiraling into something more concerning. They were concerned her instability at that time made her untrustworthy. I went along with what my team told me to do because I was a minor and didn't want to create any more issues. Britney learned of the pregnancy when the article was released. To this day, the hurt of not being able to tell my sister myself lingers.

I was still suffering with morning sickness, which in a way drained me of any fight I may have had at the time. I was banished and basically hidden away. Misery and loneliness persisted. Those feelings intensified when the team decided Momma and I should be moved from our house to a secure location far away until *OK!* released the story. This irritated me, yet I still couldn't garner the strength to object. Supported by our security team, my mom and I traveled to Connecticut, or so I was told, to an undisclosed location. We flew into New York and then drove for what felt like hours. To this day, I'm not sure where in the Northeast we hid.

Thanksgiving 2007 was spent in a small cabin without the tradition that the holiday inspired. There wasn't a home-cooked meal surrounded by family and friends. Morning sickness became more like an all-day affliction. The cold weather was unbearable and kept us from even sitting outside. Staying in that cabin was insufferable. Momma wore her disappointment like her favorite jacket, and only Sugar, my bearlike lovable security guard, showed me true compassion. I'll never forget the many movies he made sure I had to stay occupied or the gold-embellished "Mom" necklace he gave me during that awful time. I locked myself in the cabin's bathroom and used one of my burner phones to call Diane, who was on vacation. She picked up despite not recognizing the number. "Diane. It's me, Jamie Lynn. I'm scared. They moved me somewhere frickin' cold. And all I know is that it's snowing. There's nothing for miles!"

We spoke for a few more minutes, and it helped just to hear her voice.

We received the news that the *OK!* issue was ready. The article, which was released in December 2007, generated epic amounts of media coverage. Every tabloid picked up the pregnancy announcement. The headlines were harsh, even by today's standards: "Pregnant Jamie Lynn Spears Not Much of a Role Model." And the television coverage was just as painful. "Jamie Lynn—no future!", "Her life is over!", and "She has no idea what she's gotten herself into." Again, I sometimes think how fortunate I was that Instagram, Facebook, and Twitter were still in their development phases at the time. Rumors spread about my pregnancy and the timing of the filming of *Zoey 101*. The media relentlessly trashed my character and speculated about whether Nickelodeon was going to air the final season of the show. To this day, a lot of people assume *Zoey 101* ended because of me or that the show was impacted in some way by my pregnancy. Nothing could be further from the truth. The final episode of *Zoey* was filmed months before I even became pregnant. When the news of my pregnancy was released, Nickelodeon supported me in my decision. The executives were only concerned for my well-being. We continue to share a professional and respectful relationship and I will always be grateful for their faith in me and the support of my family.

My baby and I were big news. Traveling through airports was out of the question. We stayed sequestered for a few more days and drove the twenty-two hours back to Kentwood to avoid the paparazzi. The cabin was bad enough, but the endless hours cooped up in that car were awful. I was uncomfortable and tried to sleep most of the way home. And still the isolation continued. This was a painful time for me. I tried not to care what Hollywood labeled me. I still felt the responsibility of being a positive role model for girls. I wasn't "America's sweetheart" or "a youth who could change the world" anymore—now words like "slut," "disgrace," and "disappointment" were used to describe me. Both my family and I were embarrassed and humiliated by every headline. There wasn't one shred of support from the press, and my story turned into an invitation for every media outlet and random person to assume they knew me, understood my motivations, or had any idea what was going on in my life. At sixteen, I struggled to make sense of everything, let alone the changes to my body and circumstance. No one on the team listened to me and I was stymied each time I wanted to speak up. This environment felt oppressive, and I started to think about doing something drastic.

I studied to earn my GED and considered my options. Everything needed to change. I was desperate to figure out how to make this new life possible and provide for myself and the baby. During the second trimester of my pregnancy, I finally felt better, and my brain could process things more effectively. No one ever tells you that the discomfort of long-lasting morning sickness makes normal functioning impossible. The relief allowed me to take better care of myself and find some joy in my pregnancy. I took time to think and established a plan. My friends stood by me and found ways to keep me sane. The paparazzi didn't make that easy and constantly hounded me.

Having dozens of middle-aged men constantly following me around wasn't simply scary, it was creepy. More than a few times we went shopping in a local store and they would follow us. Some of the more reprehensible photojournalists would shout questions at me like, "Aren't you ashamed of yourself, Jamie Lynn? How does it feel to be a disappointment?" As many as ten at a time continued to follow me when I went on errands and even to my doctor's appointments. They published pictures of the clinic's name where I received my prenatal checkups. The truth—going anywhere was taxing and staying home was claustrophobic.

While I was considering my next move, my parents, still desperate to retain control, tried to convince me that Casper should remain my ex. They told me I was living in a fantasy world if I thought he was going to be a loving and supportive partner. That I needed to get a grip on reality and he was going to ruin everything I had worked so hard for. They may have been right about this, but I wasn't ready to admit that Casper was of questionable character—not even to myself. At that point, I wasn't having it. I was so caught up in making the perfect life with Casper and our baby. They had little faith in my ability to establish a healthy environment and happiness for myself. Their cause became less about the baby and more about the financial security of my future.

Ms. Lou Taylor had staunchly defended me in the midst of the turmoil. She had become a part of my team two years earlier, and I grew to trust her to oversee my interests. But Ms. Lou had a vested interest in keeping me profitable. As my pregnancy progressed, Ms. Lou became a mentor to me, teaching me financial planning and budgeting to keep me solvent. Previously, I had not been involved with how much money I earned or how it was invested. But now, everything was different, and as much as I would have loved a supportive partner during this critical time, Casper was indifferent to planning for the future. Don't get me wrong—he loved the creature comforts that came with being in my life, he just didn't want the responsibility.

I once again turned to my friends, especially Diane, who helped me sort through the issues I needed to resolve and establish myself as a strong independent young woman. Using the burner phones, she and I had several conversations, developing a long-term plan. She helped to arrange a meeting with a lawyer from Hammond, who was outside of the team, to determine steps to emancipate myself and take ownership over my life and finances. There were too many people around me telling me what was best for me, and I wanted to make my own decisions. At sixteen, my impressionable heart had already woven dreams of a home where Casper and I could raise our baby and prove we could be happy. The only way that could happen, and fast, was to move out from underneath my parents' roof and be on my own. Resistance to this idea came quickly from all fronts. My momma and daddy thought I was being foolish, and my brother, Bryan, felt sad that I was dealing with such weighty decisions at my age. Britney was in the midst of her own crisis, and because we were isolated from each other, our communication was nonexistent. My family denied my attempts to be independent and left me with no other choice than to threaten to file for emancipation with the courts. I spent days agonizing with my pending decision. But I followed my gut and instructed my new lawyer to go ahead and draw up the petition. The following Saturday morning, my lawyer and I showed up and served my momma with papers. Daddy was gone at that point, and Momma contacted the team to discuss the issues. They had real concerns about me marrying my boyfriend and giving him access to all of my earnings. Simultaneously, my sister was experiencing her own breakdown, and media speculation about her wellness and our family already had the paparazzi swarming. Everyone involved with my saga reluctantly agreed that we needed to do what was best to avoid any more negative media attention.

CHAPTER 6

Breaking Up and Letting Go

Trying to gain my independence by threatening Momma with emancipation papers felt foreign to me. However, I needed everyone to take my concerns seriously, and this felt like my only course of action. When my lawyer and I showed up to serve her, Momma stood there in a state of disbelief. We both were probably thinking the same thing: How did it come to this? We waited while Momma called the lawyers and conferred with my team. In the end, they decided to do what it took to protect me. Emancipation would put me at risk in personal and financial ways no one wanted. We trashed the emancipation papers, and I was given my independence. Our agreement granted me the freedom to manage my own affairs and make decisions for me and my baby. My parents would still be my legal guardians and have the authority to step in should I make poor decisions. I had no intention of making a mess of an already tenuous situation. I knew in my heart I was making the right choice, but gaining my independence came at a price.

The events of the day were emotionally draining, and our mutual feelings of discomfort made it impossible for me to stay in the house any longer. Momma wanted me to continue living with her, and she wanted to help me navigate the next year of my life. But I just knew that if Casper and I were going to have a chance to be together and raise our baby, I needed to move from underneath her roof. As good as Momma's intentions may have been, I would never be able to assert myself and grow into the mother I wanted to become living there. With my head held high, I marched myself to my room and threw everything I could into large garbage bags. The shabby plastic bags stuffed into my Range Rover were a comical sight. I drove out to Liberty to stay with Casper at his family's home.

At first, he made sincere attempts to be supportive. But we were young, and Casper was more interested in his friends and having fun. Sometimes he would say just what I needed to hear, but I'm not certain he had any real interest in taking on the responsibility of building a life with me. The truth was, regardless of my love for him, Casper's past indiscretions undermined my faith in him. I had a niggling feeling he wasn't good for me or the baby, but Momma wouldn't have conceded to letting me move out if she thought I was going to be on my own. In my young heart, I honestly hoped it would be a new beginning to our relationship. Now that the most difficult decisions had been made, I felt compelled to show the world I could do this—be the "perfect" teen mom who made it work and built a steady relationship with her boyfriend. We weren't going to be a statistic. We were going to make a family for our daughter.

I did everything to prove my devotion to him. We "played house" in his parents' home and tried to be a family. From the onset I knew I wanted a home of my own but agreed a few weeks in his home would give us time to plan. Initially he was working in a welding job, but he quit soon after I moved in. Within weeks I found a small bag of pills while cleaning. I didn't recognize them and without much thought, I flushed them down the toilet. I called him and casually mentioned that I'd gotten rid of some pills I found in a baggie, and he flipped out. He was spitting mad, saying they belonged to a friend of his. Genuinely concerned, I appealed to his mom, asking questions about his habits, and she basically said, "Boys will be boys." Ribbons of doubt began to unfurl. Strike one.

Life in that home wasn't good for me, but my pride demanded I smile for the world. Out of necessity, I developed a character I performed for everyone. "Happy Jamie Lynn" wore a cloak of well-being that shielded the anxiety and unease I experienced on a daily basis. Casper's parents were pleasant, but their permissive ways made me uncomfortable, and we didn't develop a close-ness. How was Casper supposed to join me in nurturing a healthy family life for us if he never had to take responsibility for himself? I didn't appreciate the paparazzi spinning salacious stories about my relationship, and I didn't want to hear "I told you so" from my parents. It was simply easier to pretend everything was good. I grew increasingly more self-conscious in his house and felt that I really needed a place of my own. It was time to move out. After a difficult conversation in which I justified the expense of a new home to my management, I contacted a Realtor and started looking at houses.

The property I selected in Liberty was in the middle of nowhere. In retrospect, that may not have been my best move. It was a quick cash transaction, and immediately I put up a high fence to secure privacy and safety for me and my growing baby. The press continued to harass me, but at the very least I was comfortable in my own home. The pregnancy had thrown me into nesting mode. I was putting together our home from scratch: everything from paint and appliances to curtains and conveniences. This was complicated for so many reasons. Primarily, because I was a child who hadn't amassed anything for a home.

Most days, Casper spent time doing God knows what, except when it came to outfitting our home with the best tech toys and televisions money could buy. He insisted on a room decked out in camouflage—bedding and all—where he displayed his hunting pictures. I went along with most of his ideas in an attempt to make him happy. One morning we were looking around our house and he said, "You know, Jamie Lynn, these floors aren't going to sweep themselves. That's something you need to do." I couldn't believe he said it and thought, *I'm paying for all this! You sweep up the freaking floors.* Realistically, what did I know about sweeping? I didn't have any experience in how to keep a house. Previously, if I wasn't working, I was at school or church or playing sports. He never picked up a broom or vacuum but nabbed any chance to spend money. I did the best I could to set us up with everything we needed while managing my morning sickness and taking care of my business affairs. I had job prospects that needed to be put on hold and I had to revamp my financial strategy to keep us afloat. When I was exhausted from the day, he went out late into the evening to party with friends and many nights never even came home.

Ms. Lou and I continued to build on our relationship, and she was a big help to me in these first months. I knew she was someone I could rely on. Her support was invaluable, especially at that time when my relationship with my folks was just beginning to mend. Ms. Lou's take-charge attitude appealed to me and was, frankly, refreshing. Her bulldozing and dynamic personality served me well at a time I came to realize that most of the women in my family struggled to stand their ground and make good decisions for themselves. She visited from Nashville to see how I was managing, and she made sure I got the things I needed to improve the quality of my daily life. She set out to make a cup of coffee and realized I didn't own a machine. When I told her the nearest place for coffee was a gas station eight miles away, she balked. Within hours, I had a French press, and she helped me make a house a home. Ms. Lou provided suggestions on decor and design, and even delivered a picture for Maddie's nursery gifted from my parents. She took one look at Casper's camouflage room and gasped. Without judgment she said, "Come on, Jamie Lynn. Let's get some stuff to refine the decor here."

With no children of her own and my unique needs at the time, Ms. Lou and I developed a rapport that went way beyond professional. I know she wanted to help in any way she could to alleviate the stress in my life. I cherished having someone in my corner whose exclusive job was to put my business concerns first and coach me on how to secure my future. But in the process, she positioned herself in such a way that made Momma uncomfortable. On one level she soothed my family's hurts and precipitated the healing process. But I got a sense that Momma may have struggled with the closeness Ms. Lou and I shared.

No one could ever take Momma's place in my life, but the previous months, the ones wrought with fear, disillusionment, and guilt, had put a strain on our relationship. Momma was conflicted; she wanted to do what she thought was right for me and still support me in my choices. And the truth is, not all my decisions were the right ones. Even when things were abominable, Momma was there with me. Throughout my childhood, I believed that to be a Spears is to be strong-willed, outspoken, and, above all, forgiving whenever possible. Grudges don't serve any of us, and it's a blessing we can disagree and still care deeply for each other. I was reared to show deference to my parents and do what I was told, at all costs. But with Froggy on the way, I started to feel a huge rift between how I viewed my family and the one I wanted to build for myself. I recognized that in myself as soon as I decided to move out of my mom's house. At that point, I didn't resent or blame them for the way I left home. I just knew I had to make my own way. As for Momma and Ms. Lou, they came together as guiding forces in my life and even coordinated the deal for Momma's book *Through the Storm: A Real Story of Fame and Family in a Tabloid World*. Still, to this day, I have not read that book. I saw firsthand the difficulties that Momma and Britney suffered after my sister read it, and I wanted to avoid the possible outrage reading her words would evoke.

The geographical isolation of the home I shared with Casper caused a rift between me and some of my friends. I couldn't hang out with them regularly and give the friendships the constant communication teens thrive on. I was moving in a different direction, and we had very little in common at that point. My life became a delicate balancing act between keeping my romantic relationship stable and maintaining my health. I wanted to believe that love between Casper and me would grow. We had some good times, but they weren't many, and his infidelity became harder to ignore. Somehow, I deluded myself into thinking if I just tried harder, I could make him happy. I pushed aside my insecurities, and I was genuinely happy when he proposed to me in March 2008. I thought, *Okay, now everything will be good.* The ring reinforced my determination that it was going to work out. The diamond convinced everyone else we were happy. The engagement proved our legitimacy to the world. I was doing the right thing for my baby.

This entire scenario was damage control for my sinking public reputation. I was still trying to be that perfect girl people had come to adore and prove that this pregnancy wasn't the disaster it was reported to be. In reality, my fiancé was gone more than he was home and his whereabouts remained unknown to me most of the time.

Some days I wanted to be with him. But wanting that and feeling secure in our relationship were two different things. At the time, I just knew something wasn't right. He wasn't acting like himself. When I asked where he'd been, he dismissed me with comments like, "Your hormones are making you crazy. I was out. Just hanging out. It was late, so I crashed at so-and-so's house." Despite the ring, trust was slipping through my fingers like sand. Strike two.

Time allowed for the strain between Momma and me to subside, and our relationship improved. After everything we'd been through, Momma was so excited to coordinate a large baby shower for me at her home. I loathed being the center of attention, but I couldn't deny her. There were false reports that I had some "redneck, half-assed" baby shower. With everything that had happened in the past seven months, with all the media coverage and negative press, it was important to me that people see the beautiful celebration honoring my pregnancy. In another attempt to control the narrative and what the public saw, I had a family friend serve as the photographer and shoot the day's events. The pictures, which were not the best quality, were sold to *OK!* magazine for an article. Reporters still swarmed that day and even flew helicopters over the yard. Everything they did was intrusive, and I felt violated during a very private time. I plastered that "Happy Jamie Lynn" smile on my face, but I started to feel a crack in my veneer. A couple of weeks later, Diane hosted a smaller shower, attended by a few close friends, where I could relax and enjoy the excitement of impending motherhood.

The countdown to my due date had begun. I felt ginormous, and my skin had stretched beyond belief. I was naive to the hormonal fluctuations that occur during pregnancy. I foolishly believed all my exhaustion and emotional issues would disappear right after the first trimester. I probably suffered from prenatal depression but didn't even know it was a thing at the time. I felt overwhelmed and did all I could to manage my anxiety. I kept busy around the house and tried to distract myself from what was about to happen. I didn't have the luxury of waiting for a natural labor to commence. An action plan was developed for the baby's birth in the hopes of controlling the day's events. An elaborate ruse was implemented to allow for privacy and security for the delivery.

On June 19, 2008, I woke up like any other day, except this morning, I was going to meet my baby. I showered and washed my hair. Youthful vanity had me straightening my hair and curling my bangs just the way I liked them. Casper and I drove to the hospital, and the 5:00 a.m. appointment time kept the media and onlookers unaware. After we arrived, I went through the typical admitting procedures I found difficult to focus on because I was about to become a first-time mom. I changed into the provided gown to start the induction process. My entire family was scheduled to fly in on private planes, which tipped off the paparazzi. This being my first baby, doctors informed Momma that it would be hours before I delivered, so the family could take their time getting to the hospital. At first, things were moving at an easy pace, and I felt as comfortable as I could. Still, the morning was teeming with drama and things moved a lot quicker than anyone expected. I was walking around to ease some of the discomfort. Suddenly the moment hit me. *Holy smokes! I'm going to have a baby.* Cupping my swollen belly, I walked into the birthing room and took in my surroundings. In an instant I was sweating and then threw up. Fetal monitors were placed on my stomach, and unbeknownst to me, I was having contractions. Maddie decided not to make us wait too long for her arrival. By the time the Pitocin took effect, my baby was already making her way into the world. Casper stood alongside me, but the birthing experience was a very personal moment for me. After a period of straining and pushing, Maddie Briann was born at 9:33 a.m. Her presence comforted me, and a message passed between us when I held her. *We got this!* At that moment the fear dissipated, and everything was right in my world.

While I was bonding with Maddie, I couldn't ignore the elements of the bizarre all around us. There were state troopers stationed outside my door and placed near the elevators. The amount of press outside was staggering. At separate times, nurses and doctors tried to come in, and I soon learned that they were reporters dressed up to gain access. Maddie was not allowed to be removed from the room. All her initial tests and checks were done bedside. Through it all I felt like it was Maddie and I facing our new world. Each time I held her I felt complete, like all my parts snapped into place. Maddie was adept at latching on for feedings and made the breastfeeding process easy. Casper was happy but used my post-delivery euphoria to ask for a new truck. "You know, Jamie Lynn, so I can drive the baby in a safer vehicle." I had already bought him a truck, and his request hurt like a physical blow. He had abandoned all sense of decency. I thought, *What a shit!* But I did buy him another truck, and by the time he put on large rims and raised the cab twenty inches, I couldn't even get Maddie in her car seat. This was another Casper con, leading to our downward spiral. Fortunately, Maddie's arrival served as a balm to my own family, and everyone, including Momma, Daddy, Bryan, and Britney, delighted in her arrival. All of us together in that room, cooing at the newest addition, brought peace to my heart—at least for a little while. I was so happy that my sister had recovered from her earlier breakdown and could share in the experience.

The parking lot was filled with press, and we knew getting Maddie home was going to be a tactical nightmare. The second part of Mission Maddie was a diversionary plan to get the press to go one way and Maddie to go the other. The problem was that for the plan to work I was going to have to let her out of my sight. Just the thought of allowing someone to hold her, let alone entrusting her to someone else, was terrifying. But I would do anything to keep her safe. Against my wishes, I agreed to the ruse. It was late in the evening. Once I was dressed and ready, I sat in a wheelchair and baby Maddie was placed in my hands. We began the slow trek downstairs to the car. The four-person team of troopers accompanied me, and before we made it to the lobby, I handed Maddie to one of the troopers and an identical baby bundle was placed in my lap. I was rolled out and a makeshift tunnel was created to protect us and ward off the cameras. I kept my head down, and gently went into the car. The door closed and I placed the fake baby bundle in the car seat. I took a deep breath and prayed that Maddie and the troopers were safely en route home. Words fail to describe my sense of relief once Maddie was back in my arms.

A few days after Maddie and I had returned home, my family went back to living their own lives, and my fiancé was back partying and disappearing for hours. Although I was annoyed by his behavior, the precious time with my baby made everything better. His absence gave Maddie and me a chance to solidify our bond, and I developed an affinity for breastfeeding. Before she arrived, I'd learned about the benefits of breastfeeding, but never imagined how reciprocal it would be. There is nothing like that physical connection between mother and child. It's so much more than nutrition. I relished the dynamic of her needing just me; that I was the only one who could care for her in this way. The sense of security knowing that Maddie returned to the safety of my arms every few hours brought me added peace. We soothed each other and shared a sense of tranquility. I spent months breastfeeding and cherishing that once-in-a-lifetime joy with my daughter.

But new motherhood was also an immense challenge. The overwhelming fatigue and mood swings faded quickly, but still, it took time for me to mentally organize all the changes that came immediately after Maddie arrived. As with so many new moms, the lack of sleep, bouts of crying, sometimes by both of us, and the first few nights all on my own made my early days of mothering challenging. I decluttered my mind and focused on our needs. I became hypervigilant in Maddie's care and established a schedule. I ate, slept, and bathed when she did. We were like one entity. It was one of the ways I maintained a sense of control.

Casper's disappearances posed new concerns about our future. The paparazzi continued their relentless pursuit of my story, and state troopers remained on our property at all hours. State Trooper Mr. Scott, whose own daughters were my schoolmates, was so concerned that his wife actually made me food. I am indebted to him for his fatherly attention during that time.

About nine days after Maddie was born, I fulfilled my second obligation to *OK!* magazine and sat for a photo shoot showcasing me and Maddie. The agreement, which was made months before, ensured I maintained some control over what was released publicly. My motivation was to keep Maddie as safe as possible with this exclusive deal. For the most part the plan worked to minimize the hysteria of the "first photos." I couldn't wait to get it over with and looked forward to getting on with my life. The shoot was as enjoyable as it could be for a new mom. Maddie was an angel, and we took several sweet pictures that appeared in the magazine. Once the shoot was completed, I was grateful for the money the pictures brought in. I had spent years earning a steady income. Now, I had no idea what was on the horizon professionally. The money would be used to support us and was placed in a trust for the future. Although cameras and media personnel continued to try and snag photos from a distance for a few months, the frenzy eventually died down.

Throughout the summer, Casper's behavior continued to decline. When we first brought Maddie home, he fussed about the curfew the troopers recommended to keep us safe. When I asked him where he was going or where he'd been, he'd simply reply, "Out." For months our relationship had been unraveling and I suspected he was doing things he shouldn't. He was moody, and I swear his whole personality seemed to change. Before Maddie's birth, he'd been gaslighting me, being evasive and playing things off as if I was the crazy one. I doubted my own sanity at times. "Jamie Lynn, I think the pregnancy is making you a little crazy." Granted, I know a lot more now about how my body changes during pregnancy than I did then. Even if I was moody, I wasn't an idiot. Casper belittled me and dared me not to believe him. He was defiant and would become indignant when I would call him out on his "overindulging." But now, he was just blatant in his actions, not even trying to deceive me or keep his activities hidden.

I realized that I was a new mom, and I had changed too. But his disinterest, lack of fatherly attention, and disregard for our needs was evident in most of his decisions. The small amount of trust I had, the hope that he would make me and Maddie a priority in his life, faded by the time fall faded into winter. Rumors began to circulate about him and other women. I was so busy being a mom, half the time I didn't pay any attention to the whispers. But deep down, I knew Casper was disrespecting me and neglecting Maddie with his behavior. And still he would feed me lines about loving me. From time to time, he would threaten to leave us if I didn't give in to his petty demands for one thing or another. He knew how to manipulate me, and I was desperate to keep up appearances.

He appealed to me to invest in his future by paying for his education. My adviser challenged this, but I insisted I do it. Two substantial installments were put into an account for him to use, and sadly, the money was gone within weeks. He dropped out of school. And despite all of this, he insisted that he loved me. The simple truth—Casper reveled in being with me for the money and everything that came with it. I couldn't see that at the time, and we continued to live in a dysfunctional relationship. I was naive and didn't know any different. With so much turmoil it was impossible to see the reality of the situation.

Ms. Lou came for a visit specifically to sit me down and present me with some painful truths. She didn't like the way things were going with Casper and felt like she needed to get me thinking about my future. "So, Jamie Lynn. What are you going to do to pay the bills—and what kind of legacy do you want to build for Maddie?" I felt like I'd been punched in the gut. Ms. Lou didn't mess around. She was direct and her delivery was intimidating. And truth was, she had skin in the game. If I worked, she got paid. But still, she wasn't wrong. When she left, I sat in my living room, stared into space, and tried to get a hold on my panic. I never had to actually consider this issue before. Before Maddie, money was readily available. I'd thought I would continue to perform on television and then delve into movies. But now, I had basically destroyed my career and lost the steady income that came with it. She gave me a lot to think about. The seeds were planted, but I needed time for them to take root.

I pulled my proverbial protective cloak tightly around Maddie. Being her mom and watching her grow filled me with such profound pleasure that at times, it became easy to ignore Casper's behavior. Unfortunately, as the months progressed, it became apparent that most of the rumors of girls and substance abuse were likely true. Aside from taking care of Maddie, my life became an intense game of whack a mole, putting out one media fire after another. There were days where intense anxiety would cripple me and the dread of what was coming would bring me to the brink of tears. To protect myself, I went on birth control, and I struggled with the adjustment. Casper once again accused me of being hormonally crazy and unstable. Looking back, I wonder if he was saying that as a way to blame me for his rumored infidelities.

The gossip about Casper's indiscretions turned factual when my team learned that his paramour was selling her story to the tabloids. A front-page article would appear within days, reinforcing my mortification and repugnance. I was disgusted with him, but just as much with myself. My team, the same people who tried to protect me from him, were obligated to disclose the explicit details of the article to me. To this day, hearing the truth of Casper's infidelity in that way remains one of the most humiliating experiences in my life. I allowed him to sponge off my hard-earned money, manipulate my feelings, and tear down my confidence. I was left with a profound sense of shame. And at that point, I still couldn't acknowledge to anyone how bad things really were. I spoke with my sister regularly and falsely assured my family that everything was fine. I was doing what I always did: made everyone believe life was good. My inner musings weren't strong enough to push my fear of public perception aside. I craved approval, and leaving would brand me a failure. But for the first time, I felt like I was outside of myself, looking down at the life I was living. I wondered if there could be something else for Maddie and me.

Maddie's angelic presence and sweet nature were the impetus to carry on the farce. But Maddie and I began spending most of our time with my entire family. We traveled together to Los Angeles to celebrate a joint birthday party for my nephews and had an amazing time. We went on tour with Britney, and the time away gave me a protracted perspective. I understood that I was more than unhappy, I was living in an emotionally abusive home and my vivacity was slowly draining away.

When we returned home from traveling, I began to make changes. I released my team, including my manager, who was my brother's fiancée. With my future business plans on hold, I continued to dedicate myself to Maddie's care. My friends, the ones who I had previously neglected, came back into my life, and hanging out with them was refreshing. Having good people in my life made a huge impact on me and soon my insecure feelings subsided.

In a final effort to get Casper help, I appealed to his family. They continued to refute my claims and brushed me off. I wasn't going to play a part in enabling his behavior anymore. New stories of infidelity and alleged drug use circulated. His interest in Maddie decreased over the months and my fear for her safety became crippling. I couldn't determine his state of mind, and the idea that his actions could harm her became a constant concern. I would not put my daughter at risk. Strike three.

I chose family and faith. I dug deep into my reservoir of resiliency. I finally acknowledged that I needed to do better, to choose better for me and Maddie. I made plans to move back to my momma's house while I got my shit together. We were starting a new life, or so I thought.

The call came late one night in April. After years of worrying that the police would knock on my door, or worse, his sister called to tell me that Casper had been involved in a car wreck while attending a bachelor party for his cousin. In the short time between my epic decision and the time I planned to tell him, my fiancé had flipped his truck and suffered substantial injuries. In that moment, unsure of how to manage my conflicting emotions—fear, irritation, and disbelief—I followed my instincts. And for a multitude of reasons, I was forced to stay beside him. He was Maddie's father, and even though I didn't see a future for us as a family, I believed in simple human decency. I would put my anger aside and find the strength to support him during his recovery. And to be completely honest, I also had concerns on how the media would report on this new development if I left: "Jamie Lynn, Heartless Teen Star, Abandons Fiancé After Car Crash" or "Insensitive Spears Leaves Her Baby's Daddy in Crisis." I hadn't endured years of anguish and sacrificed my self-respect to protect my public image just to destroy it now. As painful as it was, I would hold off on leaving until Casper was back on his feet.

That decision, though made immediately, was problematic. I was already checked out of the relationship and moving on. It was difficult for me to care for him because I was full of rage and frustration. His months of betrayal and neglect left me resentful of the care I had to provide. He knew I wouldn't leave him during such a difficult time and as his condition improved, he took advantage of my kindness. The stronger he became, the more powerful my bitterness and annoyance grew.

The accident gave Casper the excuse he needed to use pain medication far more than necessary. As far as I could tell, he was a very lucky man to still be alive, and he could use this time to get on the right track. But he didn't. Maddie and I stayed for months while his strength returned, but soon the old habits of deception and daylong disappearances reemerged. When the situation became intolerable, Maddie and I spent time with my friends. When we needed to get away, my sister's tour gave us the excuse to leave town. The more time we spent apart from Casper, the better our lives became. As

Maddie blossomed, so did my inner strength. We deserved better than an absentee father.

Sometimes when being in Liberty was overwhelming, Maddie and I would spend a few days at Momma's house. She always welcomed us, and the reprieve from the insanity helped me gain further perspective. I loved being with my good friends Brandi and Diane and being around my extended family too. I was happier, and Maddie loved being surrounded by people who adored her. We were both getting exposed to new people and opportunities for joy.

The Mitchells were hosting a baby shower for my cousin Laura Lynn. (The Mitchells were the parents of Brandi's boyfriend, Dane.) Toward the end of the afternoon, Dane and Brandi stopped by to say hi. They pulled up in a black Escalade, and I stepped up to peer inside. They were drinking snowballs, a kind of shaved ice confection. I stood there in my gray turtleneck dress with Maddie on my hip. Brandi said, "Jamie Lynn, this is Jamie Watson." I knew Jamie was Dane's best friend, but not much else. He said hi. That was the first time I laid eyes on him and didn't think much of the encounter. I was aware of who Jamie was through conversations with Brandi. After that introduction she started to mention him more. Jamie had started his own IT business that had grown rapidly, and he was a big deal around town for being a successful self-starter. His work took him all over the country, and I could relate to his transient, independent lifestyle. I appreciated that Jamie was an adult who had his shit together at a time when my fiancé was focused on getting his next fix. Brandi kept on dropping hints that he was someone I should consider getting to know, but my mind wasn't there. Every time I went to hang out with Brandi, Jamie would show up more and more. But still, I didn't think much about it.

A few weeks later, Brandi sent me a text to stop by Dane's on my way home. I pulled up with Momma and Maddie in tow. Jamie and Dane were putting themselves on display as they worked out. I swear Jamie was trying to impress me—but he'll deny it! We said hi to each other and smiled. The whole exchange was less than five minutes, and I drove off thinking about all the difficulty I was experiencing with Casper.

Once again, I realized I needed a few days away from Casper and the isolation of being in Liberty. Maddie and I went back to Momma's. I began to spend even more time with Brandi and her friends. It was refreshing to be with interesting people from all walks of life who had professions and ambitions. They were older than me, but the age difference didn't separate us as a result of my own experiences. The more time I spent with Brandi, Dane, and their group of friends, the greater the disconnect I felt with the life I had in Liberty. But within a few days, I went back.

In early October, I suffered a bout of debilitating congestion and bruised eardrums after taking a flight. An invasive sinus surgery followed as a result of these complications. Momma took charge of Maddie, and Casper was responsible for getting me and my medication home after the procedure. He managed to set me up in bed and then immediately helped himself to some of my pain meds and took off to party with friends. I was so out of it that his behavior didn't faze me. Momma was furious.

After the surgery, I was extremely nauseated and suffered a lot of pain resulting from an irritating drip that ran down my throat. I thought about how Casper basically abandoned me and felt more resentment after everything I had done for him. I spent a few additional days recovering and started to feel more like myself. Brandi and I were going to a wedding for a friend, and she asked if I would be willing to come along with her to New Orleans for a work event for Dane and Jamie. "Please, Jamie Lynn, I don't want to be the only girl. And you know Jamie really likes you." I tried not to think too much about her last comment and decided a night out was just what I needed. Jamie picked us up in his Porsche, which I think he did to impress me. Sports cars weren't my thing. They still aren't. I much prefer a big, spacious truck. The four of us spent the drive casually talking. Jamie and I had a great time at the party goofing around and daring each other to do silly things. I think both Jamie and I really saw each other for the first time. Not the childhood actress and successful businessman but our authentic selves. It was the first night I had ever gone out for a night of pure fun, and as platonic as it seemed, I kept wondering if I was doing anything wrong. Casper and I weren't together—but we weren't officially over either.

For the Thanksgiving holiday, Momma, Maddie, Casper, and I flew to New York to celebrate with my brother and his family. I was still experiencing residual effects from the sinus surgery and Maddie caught a cold. Casper was simply miserable. He no longer enjoyed spending time with us, and it was obvious he just didn't want to be here. He was complaining and asked if we could cut the trip short. I texted Brandi: *I've got to get out of this. It's awful. He's miserable and so am I. I just can't be around it anymore.* After returning to Louisiana, I knew our relationship wasn't working. But even though we had separated, I mailed out the family Christmas cards I'd ordered back in October—trying in vain to keep up appearances.

Just weeks into my sinus recovery, I found out I needed to have my wisdom teeth extracted. Momma insisted Maddie and I spend the month of December at her house so she could help me recover and we could enjoy the holidays. The procedure went well, and I spent a few days recovering. Outdoors, Mother Nature had surprised us with a preholiday snowfall. Snow in Louisiana is rare, and Brandi called and said they were driving around enjoying the spectacle and wanted to stop by to see me. By now I knew "they" included Dane and Jamie. If you've ever had your wisdom teeth pulled, then you've experienced the nasty taste inside your mouth and the overall icky feeling as you heal. But I didn't think about how I looked.

The three of them came into the living room and found me sitting on the ledge of the fireplace. Dane and Brandi sat in the two-seater sofa, which left three other places for Jamie to sit. But instead, he lay down on the floor at my feet. It was so peculiar, but he seemed so at ease there. We all just smiled and laughed. After a while, they left to enjoy the day.

Once again, the Mitchells were hosting a party. The holiday festivities were a tradition, and Momma was happy to stay home with Maddie so I could go and have some fun. She didn't have to offer twice. I walked into the party and saw Jamie before he saw me. I got that butterfly feeling in my belly and thought, *He kinda likes me and I just might like him too.* He was in the kitchen making a drink for another girl. As I made my way to my friends, I called out, "Hey, Jamie. Come over here and bring us a drink." And he did. We spent the rest of the night hanging out and flirting in a fun way. I remember thinking how nice it was to be out, enjoying the attentions of this successful, well-intentioned man who was solely focused on me. Jamie was fun and nice in the best way possible. We talked and laughed, and I couldn't help but consider the vast differences between Jamie and Casper. I had me a bit of a crush.

There were lots of parties throughout the holidays giving Jamie and me opportunities to spend time together in groups of people. We exchanged telephone numbers and started texting. We still hadn't been on a date yet, and the no-pressure time we shared worked for me. Maddie was my number-one priority and Jamie respected me for it.

Brandi invited a bunch of us to come over to Dane's and hang out. I came with Maddie and, of course, Jamie was there. We all sat around on a big couch and Maddie played at my feet. The scene was casual, and Jamie sat opposite me. Maddie, who was typically clingy, took to Jamie right away, and he adored her in kind. There was something so easy in his nature that called to me and, more importantly, her. He had a goofy confidence that made us comfortable around him. Jamie was amiable and just an all-around nice guy.

We continued spending a lot of time with our group of friends, but neither of us was ready to officially date. Our romantic feelings, the ones we worked to keep contained, came second to the relationship Jamie, Maddie, and I shared. He was incredibly patient, which only made his appeal stronger. The slow burn of our relationship gave me time to get comfortable with the idea of us. I found the more time I spent with my friends, those crazy insecure feelings instilled in me began to subside. I wasn't crazy or paranoid, I realized.

By the end of 2009, I felt confident my obligation to support Casper's recovery was over. Maddie and I officially moved out of the Liberty home. Casper spent months in a downward spiral that had nothing to do with the accident and everything to do with the substances he had become dependent on. All of my attempts to help him were ignored and the volatility in our lives became intolerable. I grappled with what to do to keep my daughter safe. Denying him visitation seemed drastic, but the instability of it all wasn't good for Maddie. Living at Momma's gave me the space to figure out what would be best for both of us. I was feeling better—moving life for me and Maddie in the right direction. I started to let go of long-held resentments and hoped Casper could discover a healthier path for himself. When I got word he was seeking professional help for his issues, I wanted to support him in a way that wouldn't entangle me in his daily struggles. The best way was by allowing him to remain in the Liberty house. Once he was in a better frame of mind and moving on, I sold the Liberty home.

CHAPTER 7

A Butterfly Gets Her Wings

Two years passed since I'd announced to the world I was pregnant. During that time, I had cocooned myself to nurture my now thriving daughter. We had spent a little over a year in Liberty, Mississippi, where I figured out how to be the mom my daughter needed me to be. But I was determined that Maddie didn't pay for my mistakes simply because I was young. I needed to break the cycle of mistrust, stress, and reconciliation. Casper's lifestyle sabotaged his ability to be a proper father to our daughter. Once we left Liberty, Casper's relationship with Maddie started to unravel. I tried to pull myself together and get on with life, but it wasn't easy for me. Panic started to set in as I realized I was a single mom, wholly responsible for my daughter's well-being. I went through an unsettling time of profound sadness that often left me listless and unmotivated. My own world had imploded, but Maddie's was just beginning to open up. Her health and happiness flourished, despite my own dismay. The mother in me took over, and I dedicated what energy I had to being the best caregiver for my daughter. I spent months in an introspective state, working through the emotional chaos of the previous years.

Learning to trust was the cornerstone of my metamorphosis. I had to learn to depend upon not just my intellect, but my instincts as well. Sometimes what appears good for us doesn't feel right. With the help of family and positive people in my life, I started to establish guidelines on how to trust others and be confident in my decisions. The complexities of being a child living as an adult exacerbated my anxieties to the point where instead of making difficult decisions, I made none at all. Both Maddie and I suffered for that. I also needed to own up to my role in the failure of my relationship with Casper. Although my naivety and youth had worked against us, I realized that holding him accountable for his behaviors, and subsequently my own, was important. I had only started to understand who I was, and even at eighteen, I had a long way to go to becoming a woman.

Being Maddie's mom and caring for her added a fullness to my life and, in turn, gave it new meaning. But there were many days she was the singular reason I got out of bed. I was relentless in keeping my shit together for her. The smile I used to wear for others was replaced by the one I wore only for Maddie. We laid low for a time to avoid the press, and I instituted an elaborate schedule to ensure that every one of Maddie's needs were met. I kept calendars and knew when everything had to be done. At the time, I was a self-diagnosed obsessive-compulsive. I never considered it a disorder because the manifestations of it made my life better and Maddie benefited from it too. She wanted for nothing. I sang to her, and we played often. Her well-being bolstered my own. Strength and confidence returned as I demonstrated my competency as a mother.

Slowly and steadfastly, joy returned to my life. The more time I spent with my friends the happier I became, and Jamie was a huge part of that. Jamie completely respected my devotion to Maddie and understood we were a package deal. Before our relationship grew into a romance, we established a deep and abiding friendship.

Diane, Brandi, and I decided to have a girls' night in. Brandi suggested we go over to Dane's family home to enjoy the pool and Jacuzzi. Sometime in the early evening, Dane and Jamie showed up. Slowly, everyone went home or to sleep, but Jamie and I stayed up all night talking. When the sun rose and we still hadn't run out of topics, I was stunned. I'd never stayed up all night with anyone. We didn't touch or kiss. But we were building a bond. I remember laughing at the thought: *My daddy's name is Jamie. My name is Jamie, and now, there's Jamie.*

Jamie quickly became a staple in my life. Jamie, Maddie, and I usually spent time in the company of friends, even as our feelings grew, to make sure Maddie felt comfortable. We were typically a threesome. We never wanted her to feel threatened by our budding romance. Early on, Jamie put Maddie's needs in front of his own and agreed she was the priority. Sometimes we would joke that he was really in the relationship for Maddie. The connection they shared was instantaneous. "Kismet" is the best word for him coming into her life. Each of us grew to care for each other, and over time our relationship evolved.

At some point, Brandi insisted that the four of us go on a double date. Everything was new for Jamie and me, and I was excited to be going on a proper date. We drove to New Orleans to see the Christmas scenery and then to a swanky hotel for drinks. On the way home Brandi and I were sitting in the back. I leaned in between the seats to change the radio and when I glanced at Jamie, he kissed me. I thought, *Oh, okay, that's weird. But okay—our first kiss.* After that, he really started to pursue me. Casper, who thought my devotion was endless, could feel me pulling away in earnest now. I started setting appointments for him to see Maddie, always with one of his parents accompanying him. Things were getting messy, and it wasn't an ideal time to start dating. Jamie wanted to take me out and I was fearful Casper would manipulate the truth and accuse me of misconduct. Jamie and I agreed that we would do all we could to keep our relationship out of the press.

But the media got ahold of the story and used a terribly

unattractive picture of Jamie and a separate one of me on the cover of *Us Weekly*. There weren't any pictures of us together, and to be honest, we weren't really serious at the time. Jamie and his friends had a good laugh at the whole thing. Our friend Peter, who has since become my second daughter Ivey's godfather, said, "Jamie. We've done some crazy shit in our lives. But you've really outdone yourself this time." Jamie's humor and authenticity were just what I needed to let love grow between us. Such a good man being placed right in front of me after leaving a destructive relationship wasn't lost on me. I just couldn't open up my heart again so quickly. But we continued to spend time together and his fondness for Maddie expanded. Feeling skeptical about bringing a man into our lives, I wasn't sure he was best for us at that point. Jamie's integrity and goodness were never in question; it was my judgment and missteps that kept me guarded. Our nontraditional courtship stopped and started a couple of times over the first year and a half.

By this time, my artistic soul was also reawakening. The sensation is akin to an itch that has to be scratched. I yearned to create and express myself. My outlet of playing Zoey was no longer available to me, and I knew portraying a character wouldn't give me what I needed at that time. I was full of conflicting emotions, and I wanted to express them. Although I'd spent years acting, music had always been a way for me to connect to my emotions.

The questions Ms. Lou posed months before came to the forefront of my mind. It was time to start establishing my independence and develop a long-term plan for my professional future. I was certain Casper was incompetent and could not help to support us emotionally and financially in the long run. For a while I had money available from my previous jobs and believed that Casper and I would share all the parenting responsibilities. But now, the enormity of the fiscal responsibility I had of being Maddie's exclusive provider hit me. I needed to take a step to securing our future. Two things came to mind: storytelling and music.

Growing up in my house, there had been music playing pretty much twenty-four seven. My momma's love of Elton John filtered down to me, and Daddy's passion for country music sparked an appreciation for the genre. During my younger childhood, women performers were releasing power anthems and positive songs. Both my sister and I loved Shania Twain—and I was a huge fan of the Chicks (formerly the Dixie Chicks), Mariah Carey, Madonna, and Janet Jackson. All of their music and experiences influenced my life, and ultimately I decided to take my private thoughts and put them to music. Country music felt like a good fit for me. I had great respect for pop music, but my songs felt more in line with my Southern roots. The progression to songwriting felt natural, yet honing my craft was a challenge.

Ms. Lou suggested I visit her in Nashville, where I could explore both my ability and opportunities for songwriting. I used one of her small offices to escape the world and focus on transforming my feelings into words. I treated songwriting like any job. I got up, went to the office, and put pen to paper. I used the quiet, introspective time to share my thoughts. After I showed my talent and dedication to writing, I started to attend sessions with other writers and industry professionals. We'd sit around in an office with our guitars and create material. These short writing trips to Nashville went on until I realized I would need to spend more time there if I wanted to continue developing my music. If I was going to give this thing a real chance, I needed to live and be seen in Music City. I knew I wanted to be taken seriously as an artist and develop strong writing relationships that could only happen if I was constantly available. A move would also mean a fresh start for Maddie and me. It would be my chance to show my daughter I was strong and capable, that I possessed the confidence to start from scratch and build a promising future. Maddie's dad wasn't going to hold us back. He was struggling with his own demons, and his visits with Maddie were inconsistent. I was still supportive of him maintaining a relationship with her, but even that wasn't going to keep me in Louisiana.

Leaving Louisiana was an unnerving decision for me. I was still learning the ropes of motherhood. I struggled with my residual feelings over the decisions and sacrifices of the past few years. My intention had been to provide a wholesome life for Maddie, but the reality was I had been scared of being on my own, and because of that, we both paid the price. That fear kept me in a cycle of behaviors that weren't good for me or Maddie. Jamie knew I needed a change, and although we would be hours apart, he understood my desire to try. Jamie flew up to Nashville with us and helped Maddie and me get settled in our new home. He continued to be supportive during a time of great uncertainty. He believed in me, and that faith served as a cushion in my life. I put our romantic relationship on hold. It didn't make sense to try and make a new relationship work with a new career, in a new city, with a young child to care for.

Brandi had just graduated from nursing school, and I offered to have her come to Nashville to help me with Maddie. I thought it was a perfect opportunity for both of us, but she opted to stay in Louisiana and make a life with Dane. I hired Erin instead, who was terrific. Soon after I paused my relationship with Jamie, Erin called to say that dozens of roses were delivered for me and Maddie. Jamie and I were both upset about the break, and a different kind of relationship evolved. We decided not to decide. We continued to talk regularly and saw each other from time to time.

Daily life in Nashville was a great kind of busy. We lived in a beautiful home in the Governors Club, and I devoted my time to Maddie and music. Maddie's days were full, and Momma came often to help out with her care. I was a sponge soaking up musical knowledge. I took guitar lessons, and I learned scales and chords and the Nashville Number System, a method used to understand chord progression. It makes playing by ear easier. I wanted to be able to comprehend the nuances of recording in the studio and working with musicians. For example, I wanted to know what "on the two" meant, and how chords were transcribed into numbers. It's similar to learning a whole new language. I practiced the guitar until my calluses developed and I became proficient in the number system. Being a part of that community of musicians brought pro-fessional purpose back into my world.

The move was a good change for us in so many ways, and starting over motivated me in all aspects of my life. I decided to challenge myself and studied for the ACT. With the number of quality schools in Nashville, I knew going to college was a real possibility. I studied for several months and felt confident that I would score well on the test. On the day of the exam, Momma and Maddie dropped me off at the local high school where the test was administered. It was a bizarre experience. I walked in with my pencils in hand and sat at one of the desks. There was only a year or two between me and the other test takers, yet I felt out of place. Within minutes, several people were turning around and staring. I heard the whispers. "Is that Jamie Lynn Spears?" "Are we on a television show?" "That's her, right?" "What is she doing here?" The sensation was surreal. Soon the proctor came in and the focus went to the exam. When the results came, I tore the envelope open with childlike enthusiasm. My score revealed I was capable of getting into a decent school. I contemplated the idea of a full-time college experience while managing Maddie and a budding music career, and just didn't see how I would be able to do everything. Maddie and music were my passions, and that was the path I chose. I believed in the value of education, but still, I had a toddler and bills to pay.

Jamie and I continued our version of a long-distance relationship for a few months, but the pressures of motherhood and working in Tennessee proved too much for me to manage. I broke it off. Jamie remained my close friend and I knew no matter what the future brought, he would be a fixture in our lives.

My assistant Erin needed to move on and my friend Kayla, who had just come out of a sour business deal, came to work for me. I loved having a friend who I could trust be there for me and Maddie. She was also friendly with Jamie, and she gave me little updates about what he was up to.

Maddie and I would make weekend trips to Momma's house in Kentwood so Casper could continue to be in Maddie's life. Casper said he was trying to get ahold of his destructive habits, and he'd sought out the professional help he desperately needed. Still, considering his past missteps and unreliability, I found it difficult to leave her with him. At this point, we agreed to supervised visits, closer to where he lived in Mississippi. Over time, Casper proved to me that he was ready to resume a healthy relationship with our daughter. I wanted so much for Maddie to have a closeness with her father I ignored the warning signs. We visited Louisiana for the holidays and Casper acted the part of father and showered us both with attention. He wanted to visit us in Nashville, and I didn't see the harm. Casper came full of enthusiasm and spent quality time with Maddie. He was helpful with Maddie and was actually acting like the father she deserved. We went to the park and had meals together. Maddie seemed happy. Initially, I saw how being a family would be good for all of us. But there wasn't a true connection between Casper and me. In fact, I felt, if not marginalized, then self-conscious around him. Despite all that, I had this thought looping in my head: *Maddie deserves a family*. After the first trip to Nashville, he talked me into more visits and, ultimately, into giving us another chance. I was once again manipulated into a place where I thought we could make this work for our little girl. He moved in with us, and within days I began to feel the same old doubts. Casper slowly revealed his true nature. He was reluctant to find work and made excuses about not being able to get a job. Almost immediately he began to undermine my rediscovered confidence. Casper would tell me how things needed to be done and would criticize the way I did things. I paid for everything, and his petty excuses for not getting work continued.

Jamie and I spoke periodically, and I owed him a phone call to let him know that Casper was back in my life. I'd put off telling Jamie because instinctively I knew he was going to disapprove. The idea of disappointing him nauseated me. Finally, I knew I had to tell him. I couldn't get him on the phone and decided to text. It started off pleasant enough, but the second I shared the news, the tone of his words changed in a way I had never experienced. Jamie's opinion meant everything to me. Anger and disappointment suffused every word. "Do you realize the mistake you are making for yourself and Maddie? He's trash. He's proved it time and time again. He's not reliable. Being with him, Jamie Lynn, is just bad! He's trash and you being with him makes you trash too. It makes me question everything I know about you."

I was hurt and his judgments caused me a lot of pain. Jamie had never been that harsh before, but ultimately it was just what I needed to hear. This time around it only took a few weeks for me to realize that Casper was up to the same old tricks. I saw through his parasitic nature and finally realized how bad he was for us. Things in the house were tense. I grew uneasy but Jamie's words gave me the confidence to end things for good. Casper said he was going home for a quick visit. I decided we would have "the breakup talk" once he returned. But within days, I knew something was wrong. Casper didn't answer when I called, and he never contacted me. I saw a posting on the social media page of a girl I followed—and there he was. Casper had returned to Mississippi and slid right back into his destructive behaviors. I didn't need to wonder about what happened any longer. More pictures and stories about him stepping out on me followed. I was relieved by Casper's departure, but the lingering humiliation cemented the end of our relationship.

I knew something drastic would be required to eradicate Casper from my life. For years I'd hidden behind a false smile and convinced the world that everything was great. Now I needed to admit to my family that nothing was what it seemed. I called Momma and said, "Casper is gone—and he is never coming back." She listened as I described some of the shrewd and twisted ways Casper had manipulated me, how I allowed behaviors that rendered us vulnerable to go unchecked. I confessed that for months I fought against every warning bell in my head to try and keep us together for Maddie. Momma told me she didn't realize until recently that Casper had grown to be utterly unreliable. She called in the Spears troops, and Maddie, Kayla, and I joined Britney on her Femme Fatale Tour. I spent the time sharing the difficult details of my life and isolation with her. Daddy, who had stepped up to help Britney during her difficulties in the past couple of years, was on the tour too. He helped get rid of the extortionists and conspirators in her life and had even committed to his sobriety in support of Britney. The conservatorship was just a small piece of his commitment to helping her. They stayed sober together, and seeing my father put Britney's needs ahead of his own desires helped my old resentments fade. For a period of time, the conservatorship mandated that Britney be drug and alcohol tested on a regular basis. My father volunteered to do it with her in solidarity. This was the first time in my life where someone was holding them accountable for their behaviors, and the perpetual anxiety I lived with for so long finally subsided. I could stop worrying about their sobriety.

We started to spend some time together and heal our battered relationship. He apologized to me for the years of humiliation and embarrassment he'd caused. He said, "Jamie Lynn. I know I don't deserve to be in your life or in that of your child. But I am hoping you can let me earn your trust again." Moving past my experiences of the previous two years helped me see Daddy was trying his best to do the right thing, and for that alone, I slowly let him back into my life. I didn't just forgive and forget. There were stipulations that included healthy behaviors and absolutely no drinking. For the most part Daddy manages his end of the bargain, until he doesn't and I have to kick him out of my life for a while.

Spending time traveling with my sister, and the people we called family, was the best medicine. The steps to be the woman I wanted to become began on that tour. It took time to stop chastising myself and start thinking in a more positive way, but somewhere out on the road I realized I'd tried everything in my power to make it work with Casper, and that simple fact made moving forward easier.

I returned to Nashville with renewed vigor. Jamie was happy to hear that Casper was gone but questioned whether I would make the same mistake again. I said, "Nope, this time it's game over." Our friendship was back on stable ground, and I focused on my life in Nashville. Jamie dated another woman, and friends set me up with men they deemed "perfect" for me. They were often professional athletes, and the dates always showed me a good time, but their notoriety didn't give us the connection my friends believed it would. One night a guy I had been out with a few times called. I asked what he was up to, and he said, "I'm out with a friend." Turned out that friend was another guy I had been out with. I thought, *Only in my crazy life.* I quickly realized going out and being seen by the public didn't thrill me in any way. I became absorbed with motherhood, writing, and singing.

Ms. Lou suggested a therapist could help me sift through the trauma of the past couple of years and my residual anxiety. I wasn't completely invested in the idea and believed I understood my depressive episodes. In the past, I'd had bouts of sadness and disillusionment that would manifest in different ways. I attributed these episodes to changing hormones and the stress of everything I endured. Until I saw some of my sister's struggles, I thought most of it was part of growing up. I was still so young, only eighteen, and until then I didn't realize the severity of the problem. There were days when getting out of bed was nearly impossible. During other periods of distress, I would completely lose my appetite and my weight would drop drastically. Talking with someone seemed to help, but the cycle would eventually return. I managed to cope the best I could and found that my creative outlet was a powerful antidote for my emotional challenges. Aside from the joy of motherhood, I'd always found it difficult to maintain a true level of happiness. Looking back, I think I spent so much time trying to be what everyone else needed, I never discovered what brought me genuine pleasure. That discovery would come a couple of years down the road.

Work brought balance back into my life. I found that living in Nashville was a big asset to a budding music career. My commitment was obvious to anyone who met me. I spent hours with musicians and other writers. I learned that there were several approaches to songwriting. I attended writing rooms, where two or more music professionals worked together for hours at a time. I had the pleasure of working with several songwriters, including Chris Tompkins. Throughout my life, I've met hundreds of famous people, but never felt starstruck the way I did when I met brilliant songwriters like Chris. Coming face-to-face with someone responsible for some of the greatest songs ever written was awe-inspiring and left me speechless. Chris cowrote award-winning songs for Carrie Underwood, Martina McBride, and Luke Bryan. He has written and cowritten "Before He Cheats," "Blown Away," and "Drunk on You." I could fill an entire page with his illustrious résumé. But like many others,

Chris made me comfortable almost immediately. He sat with a guitar and asked me to tell him a story. He'd strum a few chords, take my words, and make magic. He told me my story was worth telling, like it was for anyone willing to share their journey. "If it happened, you can tell it." My history was the soundtrack to my life. I spent months sharing parts of myself and writing music that exposed the most vulnerable sides of me.

I also worked with Liz Rose, one of the most respected and celebrated songwriters in country music. She had written award-winning songs for Taylor Swift, Miranda Lambert, and Carrie Underwood. She had won an Academy of Country Music award and been nominated for multiple Grammys. I was honored and humbled she saw potential in me and was willing to work with me. Liz was knowledgeable and I found the experience inspiring. She was wonderful to work with and encouraged me to continue when I got dismayed. Until I started writing, I didn't realize how some songs could come in minutes and others would force me into a journey of profound self-discovery and challenge me on an emotional level. With making music, it's all me—the raw, blemished, and imperfect me. My fans hear the finished song, but they don't know the inspiration or the hours of writing and recording that went into it. Once the song is released, it becomes subject to others' interpretations. My song becomes theirs, and if my vision gets lost along the way, well—it's a natural consequence of sharing music with the world. Music transports all of us to another place and time. It evokes memories and emotions in a way no other medium can.

When I wasn't caring for Maddie—nurturing, having playdates, or attending to her needs—I was laser-focused on writing and performing. Like all Nashville musicians, I paid my dues playing gigs at small venues. I shopped my music around to a few labels, who indicated I should keep at it—so I did. I kept writing and performing. I sang at a few of the honky-tonks and bars on Broadway.

In between performances, Maddie and I traveled home to Louisiana to see family. Visitations between Maddie and her dad dropped off month after month. It is well documented that Casper struggled with drugs and alcohol and encountered difficulties with the law. He couldn't make child support payments. His interest in her waned. The parental bond between father and daughter was collapsing, and I felt compelled to do everything necessary to protect my daughter. I appeared in family court a few times to safeguard Maddie's interests and was eventually awarded full custody. I continued to encourage supervised visitation between Maddie and her father. The judge ordered him to be drug tested before spending time with his daughter. He balked at the concept, and at times didn't bother to visit at all. His parents wanted to maintain a healthy relationship with Maddie, but their son always came first. I came to distrust their ability to put Maddie's safety first, and over time that relationship began to dissolve. I was determined to provide opportunities for Maddie to see her father, but only if everyone adhered to the court-mandated guidelines.

The chaos back home wasn't going to sabotage all the hard work I'd put into making music. I'd dedicated the past couple of years to fine-tuning the art of songwriting. I was introduced to many music professionals and decided to work with a producer who put together a fantastic band for me. I was proud of the music and began to perform the songs live. In the beginning, I was skittish about baring my soul to the world night after night. Each song takes me to a specific place and time in my life, that sometimes leaves me feeling raw and exposed. As weeks passed, adjustments were made to the arrangements, and I just accepted the changes. They were still my songs, but something felt off. The music professionals I thought understood me began to make additional changes to my style and how I carried myself onstage. I had immense respect and appreciation for the advice given to me by the people around me. At an earlier time in my career, I may have been able to agree to these changes. But now, I'd had a fundamental shift in how I wanted to present myself, and I just couldn't be what they envisioned. I began to feel like a puppet or that I was participating in a country music star summer camp. Nothing felt right. My irritation grew, and I became very robotic in my response to the environment around me. I felt like a product, not myself—a doll designed to look the part. It left me hollow and uncomfortable. I couldn't reconcile their creation with the very personal nature of my music. None of it felt authentic to me. Was I not enough?

I began to doubt myself, and that triggered a heightened state of anxiety. I once again lost control over my own decisions and felt adrift. The time and money I poured into the production wasn't yielding the results I wanted. More importantly, I felt stifled and uncomfortable in my own skin. This all came to a head when a performance was scheduled for a number of industry insiders, select fans, and invited guests. Originally, I was told that many of my fans, both domestic and international, would fill the venue. There is nothing like walking out onstage to a crowd of supportive people. But at that point in my life, I was already feeling vulnerable, and as I approached the mic, the lack of positive energy in the room disarmed me. I felt like the attendees were waiting to be wowed. The pressure was overwhelming, but I was trained to push through and be the best I could be in these moments. My band and I started the first song. I had to stay hyper-focused to get through it, when historically performing was automatic and fluid. The crowd warmed up a little, but internally I was unraveling. Something was happening. As the music for the third song began, the words and timing dissipated like smoke rising into the air. I managed to fake my way through the performance. However, for the first time, I rushed—quickly closing the end of the song. The expectations placed on me as a child performer had always motivated me to be the very best in everything I did. I am a Spears, and nothing less than perfect would do. That pressure, which many times had served me in a positive way, began to undermine my confidence and ability. I was scared. Thinking about what went wrong after the show, I convinced myself that the appearance was poorly planned and hadn't been what I had expected.

Sadly, the panic grew with each passing day. The tipping point came when the band and I were practicing in the studio. The producers and my dad were there as we ran through the songs. The pressure of having Dad in the room may have contributed to my already building anxiety. I always wanted to be the best at what I was doing, every time. The session should have been easy, fun even. But I was too much in my own head, second-guessing what felt right. Here I was, singing my own words, sharing my own stories in a way that felt all wrong. In the midst of singing and knowing I was being evaluated, a sudden and powerful sensation overtook me. A crippling stage fright like I had never known struck me. I never really had anything like it. The closest thing I experienced to that was the overwhelming self-consciousness I felt during high school whenever I played sports, anytime I took the field or got on the court. I was like a human lightning rod. I didn't want that kind of attention or to be ridiculed for my performance—so I became a cheerleader. This was different. My brain felt like a computer going dark, everything shutting down. The anxiety of the moment manifested physically, and I grabbed on to a table, fearing I was going to pass out. I made my way to a couch and Dad sat alongside me. I was still dizzy and couldn't remember if I had anything to eat that day.

My dad looked me in the eye and said, "Jamie Lynn, you should go home and get things right." I knew he was correct. I needed to slow things down. I desperately wanted to go home to Louisiana as soon as possible. I learned early on that a strong woman, a courageous one, recognizes when she is in over her head.

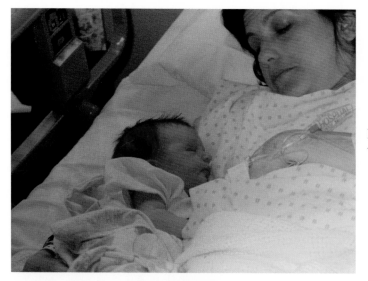

Mom and me
when I was born

Me and Daddy

We were always flying somewhere.

Me, Brit, and
Mom when
we lived in
New York

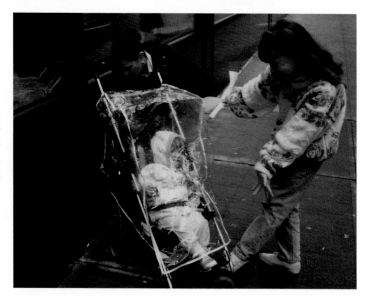

Me, Mom, and my brother, Bryan, in New York. Brit is taking the picture.

Brit doing my hair for school

When we lived in Florida for the *Mickey Mouse Club*

Me, Laura Lynn, Brit, Ryan Gosling, Justin Timberlake, and TJ Fantini during the *Mickey Mouse Club* days

Me and my friend
Crystal giving Mom
and Brit pedicures
on a flight to
who knows where

Mom and Brit reading
while getting pedicures

Backstage at the 2002
Teen Choice Awards:
Laura Lynn, my friend
Crystal, Reese Witherspoon,
me, Selma Blair, and Brit

Walking out after
Britney's wedding to
Kevin Federline.
The press and curious
onlookers were waiting
to get pictures.

Me, Mom, and Brit at Britney's baby shower, 2005

Mary-Kate and Ashley Olsen, me, and Aaron Carter backstage at a show of Britney's

Goofing around with Maddie, age three

Me and
Maddie

The day
Jamie and I
got engaged

Our wedding

Performing

My niece Lexie's birthday in Malibu. The whole family was there.

These are the two first responders who saved Maddie's life, so we invited them to her birthday a couple of months after the accident. It was extremely special for them to see her alive and well, because the last time they saw her she was in a helicopter on life support.

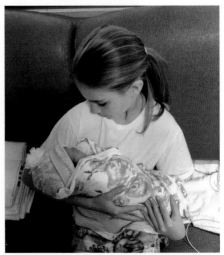

Maddie's first time holding Ivey

The family at one of Maddie's softball games

Mom, Brit, Ivey, and Maddie just hanging

Packing the kids up to go shoot *Sweet Magnolias* with Netflix

Maddie duck hunting with her cousins Preston and Jayden, Britney's sons

Easter lunch after church, 2021,
at Jamie's parents' house

Easter happened to fall on my
thirtieth birthday in 2021.

Ivey's third birthday party had to be
small due to COVID, so we had
a princess tea party with our family,
and Ivey and Maddie both got to
invite one friend. Maddie, Mom,
Ivey, me, Nana (my mother-in-law),
and Maddie's friend Raelyn.

The family at Ivey's third birthday

CHAPTER 8

Much More Than the Right Guy

I left the studio, made a few calls, and packed only the essentials that Maddie and I needed. I was normally so organized and efficient, but my lack of focus now was just another symptom of a much bigger problem. Tickets were coordinated. We were on our way to the airport and headed for the comfort of family, friends, and familiarity. Instinctively, I knew the support and peace of home would provide the relief I so desperately needed. My momma would be there to help with Maddie and give me the time I needed to recuperate from the angst and agitated state I was in.

On the plane ride home, I had a chance to collect my frantic thoughts and try to make sense of where everything went wrong. Perhaps it was a result of my upbringing or my experiences in the entertainment industry. The slide into disillusionment started with my trepidation about changing so many aspects of my performing. I went to Nashville with a concept and had felt really good about where I was headed. My songwriting allowed me to connect to my innermost thoughts and reveal myself in a completely new manner. I was naked and exposed—free to be me. But when people started to layer me with production, presentation, and style changes, it just felt wrong. Their concept contradicted every notion I had of myself. None of that was good for my mental health. I craved control and needed to chart my own course.

One of my first instincts was to call Jamie. We'd spent the past few months talking frequently and I knew in my heart he was going to be there for me. He has always been a source of comfort for me. When Jamie picked up the phone, he could tell instantly that something was off. Jamie was amazing to me; he brought humor and levity to the heaviness of my situation, by saying things like, "Jamie Lynn, yeah, you're nuts—but all the good ones are. And you know what? That's okay." He never made me feel awkward and his understanding made me feel normal.

I stayed at Momma's while I was back home. Within a few days, I knew I needed professional help. I was no stranger to anxiety and panic, but my previously mastered coping mechanisms weren't working. Unlike the Nashville counseling sessions, I knew I was going to have to be invested in the process if I was going to get through this. In all honesty, with other doctors I basically told them what I thought they wanted to hear. In the past, a counselor would ask questions and validate my perfunctory responses. I wasn't willing to dig deep and reveal the demons that denied me my happiness. For years I believed I was managing, and I was still in the cycle of pretending everything was fine. But I was scared by what happened in Nashville and spooked by some of my sister's behaviors. I didn't want to slide into a place I wouldn't be able to pull myself out of. I sought out a professional I had confidence in to provide guidance and insight. I chose a new psychologist in Louisiana, who I felt comfortable sharing painful and personal details of my life with that I had never expressed before. This time felt different with my family and Jamie to support me. I was finally ready to open up and get to the root of my difficulties. I was officially diagnosed with anxiety, depression, and obsessive-compulsive disorder. Up to that point, I managed well enough. But then, the culmination of everything—pregnancy, public humiliation, stress, failed relationship, et cetera—was too much for me to handle. It took a lot for me to keep it all together. I committed myself to regular sessions and I quickly felt the positive effects of being home and quality therapy. I was on the right track. My hope was to spend a couple of weeks recuperating and return to Nashville, refreshed and ready to record. Then life threw me a curveball in the form of a broken bone.

One thing about Momma's house that made me crazy was the lack of a good Wi-Fi signal. One day I had some emails to follow up on and knew the only way I was going to get a decent signal was to go outside to the second-floor balcony that was just off the bedroom. I went out the door, and by the time I remembered the door automatically locked when closed, it was too late. You can ask anyone who's lived in that house about that balcony door. At first, I wasn't concerned because the balcony had a glass wall that overlooked the living room, where I knew Momma and Maddie were playing. By the time I finished handling my business, I peered through the glass and found the living room empty. Impulsively, I decided to climb over the balustrade to a lower wall and leap down. Well, the physics of my plan failed, and I jumped twenty feet and fractured the bone in my heel. That fracture changed the course of my life.

After I had gone to the ER and had gotten X-rays, the doctor prescribed a boot for my broken heel, and I was laid up for several weeks. Of course, this limited my mobility and driving habits. Momma was exceedingly helpful with Maddie. I was forced to take it easy for a while, and except for going to my therapy appointments and the occasional outing, I spent most of my time healing from my injury. My days were spent on the couch, and Jamie devoted all his free time to me. Other than my daughter, being with him was the only thing that felt good. He was a curative. Jamie would bring me food and, even better, conversation. We spent that time really getting to know each other on a deeper level. I finally let him in, to truly know me. He was sincere when he said that was all he ever wanted. Most days he would bring movies. Jamie introduced me to iconic and classic films. He insisted that we watch all of *The Godfather* movies. He would start the movie and within a few minutes we'd be deep in conversation. Something would spark a topic, and soon the movie was forgotten. There was the occasional nap too. To this day, I have yet to see them in their entirety. Jamie ensured that I laughed often and didn't take my struggles so seriously. He even drove me to my doctor's appointments and took Maddie for ice cream to keep her occupied. It was strange that he'd keep Maddie preoccupied with treats while I was trying to keep my world from collapsing. He and I were in the beginning stages of exploring who we were to each other, and his willingness to walk that road with me and Maddie felt surprisingly profound.

My therapy appointments were crucial to helping me move into a healthier period of my life. Connecting with the right therapist made all the difference. My psychologist suggested I try medication to ease my symptoms while we worked through the root of my challenges. The meds did more harm than good—they made me exhausted and apathetic, and functioning day to day became laborious. At times I could barely muster the energy to get out of bed. Per my doctor's recommendation, I remained on medication for months, and much to my dismay, it failed to remedy my issues and made others worse. Talking about the anxiety was the most beneficial, and pharmacological support, while effective for many, didn't work for me. Talking freely about my anxiety eased my way to communicate my needs and wants. I was just discovering how freeing it was to share my truth and my burdens. Acknowledging I wasn't happy with my professional circumstances was the first step to making radical changes in my life. Sharing my thoughts with Jamie further validated the concepts I had for my career.

Our feelings for each other grew over time, and Jamie's genuine concern and support of my well-being was the catalyst that expanded my love for him. His unconditional love for me—just Jamie Lynn, not the performer or the celebrity—healed a part of me that medicine or therapy couldn't. He helped me understand that just being me was enough. I took that lesson and allowed it to permeate every aspect of my life. I started to think about how I wanted to live and what would make me happy. The instant connection between Jamie and Maddie grew stronger the more time we all spent together. Jamie was devoted to both of us. I think I fell more in love with him because of his love for Maddie. He said that the kind of mother I was made him love me more. Although our relationship wasn't love at first sight, I think it may have been fatherhood at first view.

Jamie jokes that when we first met, he had no idea who I was. Obviously, he recognized my last name, but knew nothing else. I took comfort in that. Jamie is ten years older than me, so it would have been weird if he were watching *Zoey 101* or followed my career. Jamie coming into our lives felt serendipitous. He understood my artist's nature and supported my career. He recently told me that the first time he saw me, he thought I was the most beautiful girl he had seen and had immediately wondered, "Why would she ever want to be with me?"

After several weeks at home, I decided to go back to Nashville and proceed to make music the way that felt authentic to me. We stayed together and managed the distance with weekend visits and lots of phone calls. But after a while that didn't feel like enough for any of us. I had become *we*. We wanted a more stable life for Maddie where she could be surrounded by family and build lasting friendships. Jamie and I wanted to be in the same city and give our relationship the attention it needed to thrive. Louisiana was calling me home. But first, I had work to do.

The period of self-discovery I spent in Tennessee culminated with me taking back my power and doing things on my own terms. I returned to Nashville and let the bulk of the production team go. We all knew it wasn't working. Everyone agreed I had the talent, and I was determined to use that talent in the most authentic way possible. The therapeutic process gave me further insight into how I could thrive in the industry. I needed to participate in the decision-making process and have control over my career's direction. Only with that control would I be able to have the career I craved. I'd spent years being shaped, directed, molded, and controlled. I'd had to do what management and my parents wanted. If it wasn't my own team calling the shots, then the studio did. Now that I was no longer a child star, I was shutting down when others tried to take control of my life. *NO MORE*, I decided. For the first time, I was ready to take ownership of my material and brand.

I picked up the phone and spoke in length to Liz Rose, whose musical insight surpassed everyone I knew at the time. But my appreciation for Liz goes beyond the professional. Liz served as a mentor and protected me from others, but mostly from self-doubt. She intervened when sessions didn't feel right. With her impressive résumé, it was easier for Liz to offer suggestions or changes. She had complete faith in my writing and performing talent and encouraged me to continue creating the format for bringing my music to the world. Shopping my music to labels led me down the wrong path— the one that undermined my autonomy. Liz and the profoundly talented producer and writer Corey Crowder laid the groundwork for my musical journey. On several occasions we discussed where I saw myself in the country music world and what would be the best way to bring my music to the people. They provided a full education on the different ways music could be released. The industry was still reeling from the introduction of music streaming services. Artists were using the internet to build audiences, and streaming services provided a new platform to showcase their music. Like authors self-publishing books, musicians now had alternative ways of releasing music. I had faith both Corey and Liz could provide the insight and expertise needed to create my album in a manner different from the ones big companies offered. Liz was living in Dallas and suggested I come there for a writing retreat. Writer Lisa Carver, whose songs have been performed by greats like Tim McGraw, Reba McEntire, and Sugarland, completed our writing circle. We spent days closed up talking, sharing stories, and creating most of the music for my 2014 EP.

We wrote and established a plan. I spent months developing a song that encapsulated what Jamie and I had experienced on the road to love. We hit some bumps along the way. After everything I had to overcome to open myself up to love, fear, shame, self-doubt, and trust, the song I wrote explained my journey in a way I hadn't been able to express before. Early on, I released my single "How Could I Want More," about being with someone who seems perfect for you, yet struggling with the inner turmoil that maybe there is something more. The last line in the song was originally "He ought to be the right guy." By the time I recorded the song for my EP in 2014, Jamie and I were engaged. And that last line was aptly changed to "I know he is the right guy."

Simultaneously, Jamie was working on a plan too. With covert help from Momma and my friends, Jamie set out to propose. He planned an elaborate day for the three of us to share. He told us to be ready around ten in the morning. Maddie and I dressed for a fun day with Jamie. I thought we were headed to IMAX to see a movie, but within minutes I saw we were headed in a different direction. Jamie knows how much I love Louisiana history and architecture, and he drove us out to one of my favorite spots. We visited Oak Alley and spent hours discovering the beauty of the structure, landscape, and stories of the area. The canopy of oak trees that make the property truly spectacular set the tone for a magical day. The massive trees provided shade and protection from the March sun. Jamie and I read about the landmark's history as we shared secret smiles and silent conversations. I sensed that something about the day was different, special even. Maddie simply enjoyed spending the day with us, holding our hands or running ahead on the vast grounds. After we finished our visit, Jamie insisted we drive to New Orleans and take a walk along the river. I almost balked, tired from the hours at Oak Alley. But he seemed so eager to go, so I couldn't refuse. He parked the car and the three of us strolled along the Riverwalk. We didn't talk much as we walked. Maddie was distracted by the people all around. Before I knew what was happening, he dropped to one knee. I was thinking, *Uh, what is he doing?* Without any preamble, he pulled out a ring and asked, "Will you marry me?" And then he pulled out another ring and asked Maddie, "Will you let me marry you and your momma?" She said, "Yeah!" and I did too. He slipped the ring on my finger, and Maddie's was a little big. We took some time to ourselves to enjoy the moment. Jamie had a photographer there to capture everything. Just when my shock was subsiding, he started to pull us along, saying something like, "Come on, we've gotta go. Everyone's waiting." Again, I was thinking, *What?* "Waiting for what?" I asked. Jamie had arranged for the important people in our lives to meet at our friend's apartment just a few blocks away. When we walked in, all of our family and close friends were there to celebrate and toast with champagne in our honor. But there was more. Momma was going to take Maddie home with her, and Jamie and I were headed out with friends for dinner and drinks. Jamie, knowing I'd been out all day, had Kayla come with a whole new outfit and stuff for hair and makeup. It was a wonderful night. Jamie planned every detail and, as I hoped, the day was truly magical.

We fell in love—Maddie, Jamie, and me. The love we share is rooted in mutual respect and appreciation for one another. We have a raw honesty that keeps us safe and leaves no room for doubts or insecurities. Together we are grounded, and I finally have the security I had been searching for after years of bouncing between my identities as a celebrity, a Southern girl, and a mom. There are times when anxiety will undermine my progress. Just weeks into our engagement, I told Jamie I was uneasy and wanted to postpone. He simply rolled his eyes and said, "I am not calling everyone to tell them that!" What he did was listen and help me reason through my fear. He was so secure in our relationship, he easily reassured me.

Until this point, I had never known true happiness. I am neither naive nor stupid. My professional life has been full of success and accolades. Those accomplishments brought me satisfaction and pleasure. But unadulterated happiness is a recent phenomenon for me. As I reflect on my past, the professional one full of money and fame, I've realized that none of that yielded the happiness I came to know once I had the confidence to make intelligent choices based upon my intuition and joy. After Maddie, I finally felt free to address my own needs—not for my extended family, team, or career. Releasing my music independently was a huge coup. Moving home felt as natural as breathing. Returning to Louisiana and building a life I truly enjoyed became my focus. Jamie, Maddie, and I began being a family. I felt comfortable working remotely, since I'd done so in the past, and I also felt confident in managing both the personal and professional aspects of my life.

The year 2014 was a big one for me. After years of trial and error, of learning, observing, and writing, I released my EP, *The Journey*. I felt a strong sense of accomplishment and was proud of the music I was sharing with the world. It's a deeply personal album where each song embodies pieces of me—my experiences and emotions infused with a soulful country sound. It's the soundtrack of my young adult life. For the first time, this music was a mirrored reflection of me, not the characters I portrayed. It was simultaneously terrifying and exhilarating. In support of the album, I needed to get on the road to perform, which included an intensive radio tour. The music business is tricky; it's not like television and movies. You've got to get in front of the right people—the program directors for radio stations. Usually, these PDs have a predetermined list of performers provided by executives who have agreements with large labels to play their artists. There's big money in music. It's typically why you hear the same thirty songs on a modern pop or country music station. But by getting out in front of audiences and meeting program directors all over the US, independent artists have a chance to build a following that helps gain the attention of radio executives. Appearing on radio shows and speaking with influential DJs can also bolster a band's popularity.

So, in March 2014, after setting off on an extensive tour, I took an extended weekend break to get married. Almost a year had passed since Jamie proposed marriage. With the impending release of my album and the travel that would be required in support of the music, Jamie and I decided we should marry prior to the tour. It was only fitting that Maddie participate as what we referred to as a mini bride. The ceremony took place on a beautiful spring day at the Audubon Tea Room and Sea Lion Colonnade. It was a beautiful affair made more special by having only our nieces and nephews serve as the wedding party. The adults sat with the invited guests as we made our vows. The reception was a scene infused with love and laughter. At one point, when we were exchanging our vows, some photographers sneaked in and tried to take pictures of our intimate moment. Security guards made quick work of tackling them to the ground and escorting them out. Jamie and I didn't even realize it happened until friends shared the details later in the evening.

Within hours of saying "We do," I was packing and hitting the road with my band. Jamie stayed behind to manage his own businesses and to help take care of Maddie. As much as possible, I would return home, or they would come to wherever I was for the weekend. From the moment Maddie was born, she had become my whole world. Nothing and nobody came before her. My own childhood experiences of being obligated to travel, the instability, and at times being left behind were still fresh. I never wanted Maddie to feel she was being cast aside or sidelined for my career. Jamie and I worked together, reassuring Maddie she would remain our number-one priority. She may have only been six at the time, but she was smart and aware of the changes resurrecting my career would bring. She had such faith in me. Maddie's youthful enthusiasm was potent and a motivating factor in my decision to do the radio tour. The strong bond between Jamie and Maddie assuaged my own doubts about leaving. I knew our extended family throughout Louisiana would be there for them should they need anything.

Road life was difficult. I missed my family and the constancy of home. There wasn't a place to cook or eat healthy foods. It was a junk food free-for-all. I preferred my early pregnancy meals of Wheat Thins with cream cheese and pepper jelly to the saturated fat and mystery ingredients of fast food. Just like filming, being on the road limits your freedom and space. I spent a lot of time sitting around in preparation for the next interview or show. I was passionate about the music and there is nothing like getting in front of a live audience—feeling their energy and receiving an immediate reaction. It was even more thrilling when people would shout out, "Hey, Zoey!" or "We love you, Jamie Lynn!" The silence that comes just moments before I begin, where the crowd settles down and prepares for me to sing, is like no other. The world stops and everyone is poised just waiting for me to start. It's heady stuff. And yet, the adoration of thousands of fans pales to the genuine love and respect that waited for me at home. I learned how fickle fans can be, and I recognized that nothing could fill my soul the way my daughter and husband did on a daily basis. Jamie and Maddie were supportive of my work and understood I had to promote my music and fulfill my dream. Jamie respected my professional goals and appreciated that I had reached this juncture on my terms. I needed to see it through. The time I spent traveling challenged my vision of my life and my priorities. Maddie and Jamie were just fine without me, and I managed without them. But "fine" and "manage" aren't fulfilling. We were a newlywed family, and I was excited to return home and be together. After the tour, I continued to promote my music, but stayed close to home as much as possible. I discovered that's where we thrived. In the years since my EP was released, I have had amazing opportunities to perform at different venues. I've performed at both the Ryman Auditorium and the Grand Ole Opry. My experiences there, singing on those stages, fulfilled a long-awaited dream. One particular night, I had just come off stage, where my dad was watching. We were smiling and enjoying the moment when all of a sudden a legend of country music came over to us. I looked up, smiling so wide it almost felt painful. I'm sure it looked that way. The man said, "Hi, Jamie Lynn. You were great out there." I think I muttered a thank-you. We took a quick picture together. As Garth walked away to take the stage, I was vibrating with excitement. We made our way to the exit and I grabbed Daddy's arm. "Oh my God, Daddy, Garth Brooks." By the time the exit door closed on us, we realized in vain that we'd missed an opportunity to watch him perform from the stage. Later I sent Maddie the picture we took with Garth Brooks and, being a huge fan of the Food Network, she asked, "Momma, isn't that Trisha Yearwood's husband? Did you get a picture of her too?"

This was about when Maddie started asking about me having a baby. I knew Jamie was on board for expanding our family, but I just wanted to take care of business and get my career moving in the right direction first. I told Maddie, "Just give me a little time, Maddie." Fortunately, Jamie continued to support me and never made me feel bad for wanting to wait just a little bit longer before adding another member to the family.

CHAPTER 9

The Sacrifice for Stardom

The glitz of Hollywood isn't all it appears to be. Being a child-hood performer is akin to being a student athlete; there is always a sacrifice, a part of yourself you give away to accomplish the goal. Make no mistake, I wanted to be an actress and entertainer. From the time I was a little girl, I loved performing characters and delighted in the response I received from entertaining anyone who would watch. My parents weren't the impetus behind my fame, but they insisted that if I wanted to act, I would put my all into developing my talent. I had exposure to the people in power in the industry because my big sister was a pop icon and cameras were always around. But just because a production assistant may have caught a glimpse of my potential doesn't mean I didn't work tirelessly to be the best at what I did on-screen.

As a young girl starting out in Hollywood, I had no concept of the universe I was entering—and I believe many of my contemporaries would say the same thing. The entertainment community and its executives operate by a completely different set of rules. It was, and still continues to be, a primarily male-dominated hierarchy that has the power to make or break any career.

Getting a job on television is one of the most exciting moments in anyone's life. Without question it is rare—like winning the Powerball lottery. But so many people don't realize the devotion, time, and sacrifice it takes to achieve such a goal. I started performing when I learned to speak. Once my parents recognized I actually had talent, they made sure I worked to improve my abilities. I took voice and dance lessons forty-five minutes away in Baton Rouge. I took headshots and went on tons of auditions. I tried out for and performed in local plays and musicals. It was the same for my siblings, whether it was sports or the arts. I think there is a huge misconception that if you are born with talent, you're guaranteed to find success and fame. I can assure you that all the young women who came up with me during the nineties committed themselves 100 percent to developing their careers.

But achieving the dream means sacrificing autonomy. I can only speak for myself; everyone's road to success may be different, but so many stops along the way are the same. As a child, I dreamed of performing and bringing characters to life. Once I was old enough to understand that I could be on television and make money, I was like, "Sign me up." But at the age of eight, it didn't occur to me that I would have to give up anything. I didn't have the maturity or foresight to know what I would have to forfeit in advancing my career. Later I would realize that I was forced to surrender control and my individuality. Immediately upon entering the entertainment world, my life ceased to be my own. I didn't know it at first because I was so caught up in the excitement of living my dream. And to be completely honest, throughout the time I worked, I was insulated from most of the manipulations imposed upon actresses. By the time I signed for *Zoey 101*, there were all kinds of dos and don'ts. Contracts include clauses that make a bunch of demands, and stipulations are usually woven into every contract. The agreements can differ from project to person. It's not quite as invasive as it was fifty years ago when studios would make you date a costar for the publicity. These days it is mostly related to appearances, promotion, and flow of information. Agreements can include things like: don't change your appearance; avoid negative press; and termination clauses for various types of infractions. As a child raised with a firm hand, I was accustomed to rules. I didn't have the freedom of time or an opportunity to do what I wanted, when I wanted. I wasn't really interested in the Hollywood lifestyle. Perhaps the consequences of Britney's difficulties with the media had something to do with it, or maybe it was that I'd started dating Casper by then.

Influencing behavior is only a small example of the clout imposed by power players. But frankly it's the intimidation and the lack of control that renders you powerless. There is a lot of "If you do this…then," or "If you don't like it, we've got someone else."

Professionalism comes before everything else, and I made sure to maintain that level of commitment. That constancy can be oppressive at times. The only reason why the public hears about the difficulties on a set or "tantrums" by performers is because at some point, the pressure of life becomes too much to manage. For women, it is so much worse than for our male counterparts. When the media reports an actor having a fit on set, they usually attribute it to someone else or say that the situation warranted the reaction. The reported list of male outbursts far exceeds the list of outbursts by women. And yet, when an actress reacts badly in any scenario, she's usually labeled a diva or unstable. The imbalance between the sexes was around way before me, and despite the efforts to right the wrongs, it still exists.

The inequity encompasses so much more than media coverage. There has always been an inherent pressure, especially for girls in the industry, to maintain their physical appearance—whether for a role, contract, or just plain vanity. As a young teen, I was fortunate I never struggled with maintaining a healthy weight, but the burden to be skinny was always there. Studios don't really want healthy and happy people; they want thin and productive ones. I was encouraged to have a trainer who didn't really educate me on the proper forms of weight management. I had others who taught me about workouts and cleanses to stay thin. I did lots of cardio and limited my caloric intake—the typical routine for those who don't know better. There were periods where I'd basically starve myself. At the 2007 Kids' Choice Awards everyone around me commented on how great I looked. My own team noticed my slim form and said, "Jamie Lynn, you've never looked better!" They gushed about my beauty and slimness. The compliments continued as I walked the "orange" carpet. People always combined the comment about my beauty with a comment about my tiny size. From as early as I can remember, the importance of looking good and being fit were ingrained in me. My parents have always been vain and believed we needed to look the part by maintaining a healthy physique. Although I never struggled with my size, I did experience periods of self-doubt, no different than most girls. But in that orange-carpet moment, with all of the cameras focused on me, I was confronted with my insecurities. The battle between loving the way I felt and the concern that I had been too big all along was raging. Executives said things like "healthy lifestyle," which in their world meant something completely different than it did in mine.

Puberty added to the pressure I experienced. When you are going through puberty, the body transforms in complex ways. Hormones are released and bones expand, creating changes both inside and out. But the studios still want you to look exactly the same. There is enormous pressure to alter your appearance—to move closer to perfect, symmetrical, and beautiful. During my teen years on Nickelodeon, I never had any procedures or injectables.

After I gave birth to Maddie, I spent months breastfeeding. She particularly enjoyed nursing on the left side, and much to my chagrin, I ended up being lopsided. My distorted breasts needed a lift; a decision made by me, for me. The doctor suggested a small implant to give me the symmetry I was looking for. To this day, I don't like the result of the procedures and what remains of my breast tissue after breastfeeding my daughters. At some point, I may have another surgery to address my concerns. I still have insecurities about my body, but the decision to fix or improve oneself through any means is different from the pressure to embark on a complete makeover to fit someone else's ideals. Even when you can achieve transformation, it's nearly impossible to maintain. But the dictates of the entertainment executives have rendered many young women, both in and out of the industry, susceptible to all kinds of physical and emotional disorders. The best example of this is still Judy Garland as Dorothy in *The Wizard of Oz*. By the time they were ready to shoot, her chest had grown two full sizes and needed to be painfully taped down. The studio required her to go through all kinds of diets and medication to remain youthful and slim. She suffered for years afterward. Audiences are fooled into thinking that a look or size can be maintained easily. This concept came full circle when Renée Zellweger portrayed Judy Garland in the biopic *Judy*. She was on a strict diet for months and actually had to be sewn into most of her costumes. Many women in and out of the entertainment industry suffer from lack of self-esteem and the unattainable beauty standards.

The power over the aesthetic can undermine a young woman's confidence, affecting career decisions and choosing what projects will best serve their long-term goals. I have seen this multiple times in my career. I have encountered brilliant professionals who had a vision that simply didn't jive with the way I saw myself. Sometimes it's as simple as a wardrobe decision or changing an arrangement on a song. I spent years placating others and doing what was asked of me professionally because I didn't feel like I had any choice. It took years for me to rediscover my power and the confidence to know that I was good enough to chart my own course.

The responsibility that comes with success and fame can be overwhelming. For me, I felt the pressure to keep a show at the height of popularity to ensure everyone had a job and got paid. I have always kept my own support team small. But the bigger the star shines, the larger the team supporting their efforts becomes. An expansive team runs the risk of employing scammers and opportunists. With so many people involved in day-to-day operations—image, finances, and care—it's nearly impossible to know who to trust. As my sister's career exploded, professionals came in and out of her life in rapid succession. Many genuinely cared for Britney's well-being and protected her interests. But she also became a target for unsavory and duplicitous people. I believe that Britney's experiences with people who only wanted to use her tore away at her ability to trust others and left her vulnerable. In the midst of all this, she'd had her heart broken more than once and become a mom. And even while she retained her iconic pop-star status, the cracks from earlier disappointments became fissures. Britney didn't reach out for help dealing with the issues she was facing, and it seemed that almost everyone on the team was more interested in keeping the money coming in than in getting her the help she needed.

I'm assuming that this, among other things, was what led to the conservatorship that was established in 2008. Lawyers and third-party entities were taking advantage of Britney's success at a time when she was suffering with what appeared to be some emotional issues. My sister didn't seem well, and those closest to her at the time, especially my parents, believed the conservatorship was the best way to protect her and the fortune she had amassed throughout her career. I think their only intent was to keep her safe at a time when she couldn't do that for herself. My father, Jamie, who wasn't a stranger to difficulties, worked with lawyers and the court to develop a trust that would serve Britney's interests. In 2008, I was sixteen years old and getting ready to deliver my first child. I knew things were difficult for Britney, but I was wrapped up in my own life. At the time, I supported her by remaining loyal to her, by listening to her and protecting her in whatever manner I could. As a daughter, I conducted myself as any well-intentioned person does. I remember what it was like to stand in opposition to my parents. In this scenario, I was simply a sister and a daughter.

Many would say my teenage pregnancy destroyed my career trajectory. They couldn't be more wrong. I believe Maddie saved me from years of potential misery. By the time I was sixteen, my siblings had already revealed the more toxic side of fame. The list of young actresses and actors who have suffered with addiction, depression, and anxiety is extensive. I suffered with anxiety and didn't realize how affected I was throughout my young life. I'm not a doctor, and don't claim to have knowledge beyond my experience. Perhaps some people are predisposed to emotional issues that are brought on by the pressures of Hollywood. Maybe imposing unrelenting demands on teenage performers who are in the midst of complicated developmental periods places them even more at risk. I don't know. I do feel that too much fame and fortune, coupled with the pressure, can lead to negative coping mechanisms that can cause irreparable damage.

My pregnancy removed me from that world at a time when I was the most susceptible to negative exposure. I escaped the added pressure from my partying peers and taking on projects that didn't feel right for me. During the summer of 2007, I was an emotional wreck. I felt powerless to the momentum of my career. Who knows what may have happened if I remained in that environment? In all honesty, the pressure and emotional volatility of being a teenager made me vulnerable. Oddly enough, Maddie brought an added sense of stability. I was forced to take responsibility for both her and me, and that changed the direction of my life and focus. Maddie became my world and being her momma made all the difference.

CHAPTER 10

The Day My World Stopped

In February 2017, my world as I understood and lived it changed. Everything I believed about life, faith, and connectedness shifted irrevocably. The news reports of our daughter Maddie's accident appeared in a succinct three paragraphs containing the cursory facts. The detailed events of Maddie's accident have never been divulged, and it is only now, after years of healing and living, that I can share our story. The memories of that day are emotional, sometimes painful, but, above all, miraculous.

Sunday, February 5, 2017, started like any other day in our

Hammond home. Sunday mornings are dedicated to family and church, but that doesn't mean it was easy to rouse Jamie and Maddie to get out of the house on time to get to service. I glanced over at the clock and groaned. "Come on, Jamie." I tapped on Maddie's door and headed to the kitchen to grab something to drink. Typically, we end up rushing through our morning routine. As I put on my dress, a camouflage design that Maddie and I both adored, Jamie reminded me that we would be going over to his parents' for lunch. "Jamie Lynn. It's Super Bowl Sunday, so I'd like to leave their house by three." He loved all the festivities that came with the big game. By the time everyone was ready to go, we were a few minutes behind. Maddie and I walked out in our matching dresses to a smiling Jamie, who sat in the idling SUV. "You girls look beautiful." He really was so sweet and it's a rare occasion when Maddie and I are dressed alike.

The church pews were full when we arrived and there was an energy of excitement that had little to do with faith and a whole lot to do with the big game later in the day. The sermon ended with "Let us pray" and a "amen." We slowly made our way out of church, acknowledged our friends and neighbors, and wished everyone a good day. A typical Sunday morning in Hammond.

One of the things we love about going out to Jamie's parents' house is that they are the most warm and welcoming people. Afternoons at Ms. Holly and Mr. J's are usually a casual affair, so we decided to go home and change into more comfortable clothes. Again, Maddie and I ended up tossing on similar sweats and shirts, both loving comfort over all else. I paused and considered not going with them, preferring to work and enjoy the solitude of the afternoon. It wasn't unusual for me to take time for myself after church. But I pushed the impulse aside and readied myself for family time. Ms. Holly prepared a roast, and the warm meal was welcoming on the unseasonably cool February morning.

After a couple of hours, I wanted to get home to do some chores and work. I looked over at Jamie and gave him the "wrap it up" sign, indicating it was time to leave. But I noticed Maddie was asking Jamie permission for something. "Please, please, just one ride on my ATV." Then she gave me her best pleading face. "Momma, can I please ride my side-by-side?" My immediate response was, "You can ride your ATV another time. I really want to get going, Maddie." Our relentless eight-year-old begged and we gave in. I told her firmly, "Maddie, just a couple of laps around the pond and then we are out of here."

Maddie took off toward the storage shed. Before I took a deep breath, Maddie was strapped in and revving the ATV's engine. Impatiently, I stood watching and thought about all the things I would do once we got back home. She took off around the pond, which had a higher water level than normal for this time of year because of a heavy rain the night before. The four of us watched in awe as our cautious Maddie, who was beaming with exhilaration, made her first loop around. Jamie took out his phone to get a video of a smiling Maddie as she zoomed by. We couldn't help but be delighted by her pure joy. The dogs were barking with excitement. Honey, the large German shepherd, known for chasing the ATVs and barking at the sound of the muffler, took off around the pond. Maddie was into her final loop, and we watched from our position across the pond. One moment we were sharing in Maddie's fun, and in the next, life as we knew it came to a screeching halt. We saw the side-by-side make a hard left turn, which caused it to flip off the embankment, and then we saw Maddie disappear beneath the water. I cocked my head to the side in disbelief, trying to make sense of what I was seeing. Instinctively, we ran into the water to get to Maddie. I heard disembodied screaming—and realized it was mine. Jamie was just ahead of me in the water, making his way to my baby. Instinctively, I ran after him. In her quick thinking, Ms. Holly called 911. My only thought was, *Get to her!* My brain shifted into autopilot, and I moved as quickly as I could. I screamed, "Oh, my baby. Oh, baby. Momma's coming! Jamie! Get to her. God! Please, save my baby!"

Within a minute, Jamie finally got to her, and I was right behind him. We clamored to pull her from under the water. "I can feel her arm. She's not moving! Jamie! She's stuck. WE'VE GOT TO GET THIS THING OFF HER. NOW!" I gulped in air and dove under, trying to free her. I started to think, *This is taking too long. Oh baby, Momma's trying.* Jamie and his dad were straining to dislodge the ATV, but it wouldn't budge. "God, please, don't take her. Maddie, Momma's here."

Mr. J screamed, "Go get the big ATV and the chain." As we continued to try and save Maddie, Jamie took off faster than a man his age should be able to and came back on a larger ATV with a chain in his hand. "Here, Dad. Tie this to the front." Mr. J dove underneath the water to fasten the chain securely to the front of it. They told me to get out of the water so they could get the ATV moved. After several minutes of effort, debilitating fatigue started to set in and my hopes we could free her began to fade. I knew that this was too long to be under the water. It felt like forever. *Oh my God!* I was crawling out of the way so the men could move the ATV off Maddie, when I saw an EMT running at full speed toward me. I vaguely thought, *Where did that EMT come from?* "Please, get here! Faster!" I panted. "Help us." Then I spoke to Maddie. "Oh baby, we're trying! Momma's here! You're not alone." The first responder got in the water just as the ATV was dragged from the pond. The ATV was on a slant, and Maddie was tangled in the protective netting. Once they freed her, the EMT pulled Maddie out and laid her down next to me. She was unconscious, her body distended, face swollen and eerily blue. I got as close as I could and repeated, "Momma's here, baby. Momma's here." The EMT started CPR. Nothing was working—not the compressions or the forced influx of air. No response. "Momma's here." Recognizing that CPR wasn't working, the EMT picked up her lifeless body and then took off as fast as possible toward the ambulance, continuing to beat on her chest. I began clawing my way up the embankment and threw up. I tried to crawl toward the ambulance, but the shock was setting in. I knew what I had just witnessed. My daughter's lifeless body. I couldn't discern time, but suddenly a fireman lifted me off the ground and he and Ms. Holly helped me back to the house. He gently asked, "Who is she to you?" and I said, "That's my baby."

He placed me on the pebble-lined driveway and I sat smoothing the rocks in a trancelike manner.

Ms. Holly kickstarted communication by calling Momma, who was in California. Even through my haze and her broken speech, I heard Ms. Holly say, "Lynne, Maddie's no longer with us." I was eviscerated by the sadness as tears streamed down my face. I rose. My baby was already in the ambulance, on her way to the hospital. I knew we had to get to her. Jamie and I shared a look. In our wet clothes and shoeless, Jamie and I ran for the car. As we pulled away, Mr. J's wide-eyed stare of devastation gutted me. Just before we hit the main road, a fireman signaled to us to stop. "They got a pulse!" We drove off knowing we needed to get to her and clinging to the hope that her heart would keep beating.

Jamie drove us as quickly and safely as possible, his view blurred by tears. We didn't say much as we drove, just occasionally glanced at each other. We pulled into the carport of the hospital's emergency entrance, bolting from the car, not bothering to turn the engine off or even shut the doors. We ran in screaming to anyone who would listen, "Our daughter was brought here. Where is she?" I'm not certain who, but I think a nurse said, "They just air-lifted a little girl from here. She's been taken to the trauma center in New Orleans." We were so confused by the timing but so grateful for the update. Jamie made a call to his business associate, Andrea, as we quickly drove to our house to grab some dry clothes. She insisted on driving us to University Medical Center. Her husband, a volunteer fireman, placed an emergency light on the top of his car and drove us the forty-five-minute ride that felt like hours. I used Jamie's phone to call Daddy and Casper's mom. My phone was lying at the bottom of the pond. Daddy had coincidentally just landed from California and planned to meet us at the hospital. Casper's mom's words comforted me. "I'll call Casper. It will be okay. We will pray for her, Jamie Lynn."

We had no information at this point. Not knowing was crippling. Jamie and I just sat and held on to each other as we cried. His tears streamed down his face as he whispered, "You should have never met me. We wouldn't be here." I had no words to give him, so I held him tighter to convey my love and support. With each passing mile, my fixed stare remained skyward. I had this dreadful feeling Maddie would think she had been abandoned—that we weren't desperately trying to save her. "Baby, I'm so sorry. Momma tried." Again, I'm not sure if I said the words out loud.

We walked into the trauma center and tried to garner as much information as possible. Moments later we were told that a nameless girl had been brought in. The nurse checked something on her computer and looked at us. "I believe your daughter is here. They are working on her now." Right there in the lobby area, Jamie and I simultaneously dropped to our knees and began praying. "Save her, God. Please bring her back to me. I don't care how or in what condition. Just bring her back." I couldn't hear Jamie's prayers over my own, but I know he was pleading for the same thing. Almost immediately, Jamie and I were taken to Maddie's room in the ICU.

The tears started anew. Maddie was intubated and endless tubes and lines extended from every part of her. There were no fewer than five machines performing different functions. But she was here. She was still here. Hope bloomed. Instinctively, I grabbed on to her where I could and held on with everything I had. "Baby, Momma's here! You're here!" My prayers recommenced—the promises, the bargaining, and the pleading. I was interrupted by the doctors, who came in to ask us questions about the accident. We told them what we could, and they provided us with her latest test results. The lead doctor spoke frankly. "We can't say much at the moment. Her scans don't show any damage or injury, but she's not responding to our pain or reflex tests. The next twenty-four hours are crucial and will tell us more." Jamie and I joined hands and began the first of many hours in deep prayer.

Jamie's good friend Dr. Donald Woolridge, a hospital radiologist, read the scans too and agreed that nothing appeared abnormal. His corroboration of the other doctors' findings gave us just a little more hope.

Daddy, whose flight had just landed in New Orleans, was the first to arrive. He was visibly shaken up as I took him to Maddie. He fell to his knees in distress and began moaning. "Oh, baby girl." He held her small hand and cried. Watching him fall apart unnerved me. Maddie brought so much joy to everyone and acknowledging the pain this was causing broke me a little more. I needed spiritual support.

"I want my priest." It came out unbidden, but it felt right.

A support team was gathering in the ICU waiting room. Dazed,

I walked into the room to thank everyone who was there. My friend Brandi explained that she had been there for a while. I looked at her in disbelief wondering how she knew what was happening. "How? I don't understand." She brought me in for a hug and whispered, "My stepdad is a sheriff, remember?" She went on to explain that he had been listening to the scanner and heard about a child, a water accident, and the location off the Fluker-Greensburg exit. "He had a feeling, because of the area reported. He verified the information and called me immediately. I wanted to be here ASAP to help in any way I can." I thought, *Oh wow, the blessings of living in a small town.*

Time is elusive in times of trauma, but at some point Casper entered the small area and ignored everything but her. His agonized expression and tears, coupled with his uneasiness, prompted me to hug him. He held me to him. "Jamie Lynn, it's going to be okay. This wasn't anyone's fault. It was an accident." Both Jamie and I found comfort in his words. Casper was clear-headed, and I was relieved I didn't have to worry about his sobriety. Daddy, Casper, Jamie, and I stood around the bed praying and doing our best just to keep it together. I got word that Father Mark was in the waiting room. The ICU had strict rules about the number of visitors. But with Maddie's unresponsiveness I demanded to have Father Mark brought in. I was so much in denial I didn't realize he was actually going to perform last rites. He anointed her head with oil and when he said, "Holy Spirit," Maddie began to thrash. Her arms and legs were flailing vigorously. I started to scream.

"Someone, get a doctor now! She's still with us." Jamie came to me, and we hugged with a renewed sense of hope. But what happened next was difficult to watch. The staff bustled in and tied Maddie down. They administered a sedative to place her in a medically induced coma to keep her from hurting herself and to allow for further healing. Her life force was temporarily extinguished, and once the nurses stepped from the room, we resumed praying. The difference this time—our words were laced with hope.

The hours of trauma seemed to last days. Maddie was motionless, but we still felt like she was with us. Casper acknowledged that as Maddie's primary caregivers, Jamie and I should be the ones to stay with her overnight. Daddy offered to get Casper a room at the nearby hotel, and he graciously accepted. They made their way out and we just stood motionless before Jamie pulled a chair as close to Maddie as he could while I lay across the foot of her bed. We waited and silently prayed. In the hospital the concept of time felt like it had expanded and contracted. Nurses seemed to come in every few minutes. Maddie's breathing machine was repeatedly checked and adjusted. Medications were administered hourly via an IV that was inserted into her neck. There was a terrible-sounding apparatus that appeared to suck the pond muck from her lungs and stomach. With each vacuum *brrrm*, I was forced to recount those minutes in the water.

From the moment Momma received the devastating news from Ms. Holly, she and Britney had tried everything to get Momma a flight to Louisiana. It didn't take long for them to realize it was

Super Bowl Sunday, and just about every private jet was chartered for the event. They continued to check for hours, and miraculously, a commercial seat opened up and Momma landed sometime in the evening. I wasn't sure of the time, only that it was late when I heard a commotion outside Maddie's room. One of the nurses was saying, "Is that Governor John Bel Edwards escorting those women?" I smiled, knowing that Momma was here. Momma's eyes went wide when she saw Maddie's little body in the bed.

"Oh, Jamie Lynn." Her pained expression deepened when I escorted her to the bed. "Look, Momma—here she is." Momma had no idea what transpired since the phone call from Ms. Holly. Momma was devastated. She was trying to stay strong, but it cost her. Momma looked from me to Jamie in confusion, trying to reconcile her grief with our optimism. "Jamie Lynn, I don't understand." As she struggled to keep her emotions in check, I quickly filled her in on the events of the past several hours. In turn, Momma described how Donna Edwards, the governor's wife and one of Momma's close friends, had arranged to meet her on the tarmac and provided a police escort to the hospital. Ms. Donna handed me an offering of blessed crosses, rosaries, and food. Governor Edwards shared some kind words: "Jamie Lynn, your little girl has our prayers and support." What a humbling moment.

After Momma visited with Maddie—crying and praying along with us—exhaustion set in and she retired to her hotel to rest.

In a kind of meditative state, I prayed throughout the night. I prayed to God and repeated the same promises from earlier in the day. *Please bring her back to us. It's not supposed to be this way. We'll deal with whatever we must to have her back. Just...please.* Other prayers came in the form of promises. *Baby, come back to me. I promise I'll give you that baby you've been begging for—just come back.* Jamie stayed up all night gazing at Maddie as if he could will her back to us. Once in a while I heard him mumble, "How did this happen?"

The next day brought more tests. She continued to lie motionless throughout the morning. In the afternoon, the doctor ordered another MRI, only this time, with contrast. The many machines and tubes made rolling her down the hall a cumbersome task. Jamie and I walked hand in hand alongside the gurney. Looks of pity came from every person we locked eyes with. The trauma unit rarely saw such a young patient and that realization reignited my fear. I squeezed my eyes shut and swallowed down the emotion. With strengthened resolve, I opened my eyes and glanced at Maddie to find hers open and fixed on mine. Breathlessly I whispered, "Jamie, look. She's in there. I can see her. She's coming back to us." The nurse noticed her attempt to rouse and readministered a sedative to keep her asleep. The act suppressed my happiness, but I understood why it was necessary. I looked at Jamie and we both smiled hesitantly. I whispered, "She's there, right? You saw her, the eye contact?" We hugged with renewed hope.

The MRI came back clear, yet doctors were still baffled at Maddie's lack of responsiveness to their tests. No one could explain it. But I saw her look straight into my eyes and connect with me.

She was coming back to us. Jamie and I resumed our positions at Maddie's bedside, praying continuously.

Everyone who was a part of our lives, from business associates to friends and clergymen, came together in support to pray for Maddie and provide just about anything we could possibly need. We had so many people working unknown to us, who provided everything from food to prayer circles for our little girl. Our families remained close by, and even though Casper had the legal right to stay by her side, he granted Jamie and me the authority to dictate visits and such. Jamie's phone had a million messages. Daddy took the necessary steps to keep the press at bay. Daddy told Ms. Lou, "It's not a good idea to come to New Orleans." My focus and energy were on Maddie. But deep down, I did still want my brother and sister there to support us. I wouldn't let anything keep me from them in a time of need, not even if someone told me it would keep the press out. Still, we could feel the love and prayers all around us. I couldn't explain the sensation, only that we all experienced a palpable energy.

Sometime around 4:00 p.m. Jamie, Momma, Casper, and I sat and performed our bedside vigil. Our eyes were heavy with exhaustion. The major tests remained negative, and Maddie was just beginning to respond to the manual pain and reflex assessments. I looked up, and my eyes widened at the laser-focused expression of attention on Jamie's face. He was looking into Maddie's open eyes. She painstakingly raised her finger with the pulse oximeter on it and pointed the small red light at Jamie. He smiled and said, "E.T., phone home." She held her finger up for a moment longer and he said it again. "E.T., phone home." At that moment I knew she was definitely coming back to us. She closed her eyes, and the nurse gave her more sleep medication. The team of doctors decided Maddie was strong enough to move to Children's Hospital New Orleans, where they could begin to assess the extent of her injuries. It seemed so quick, but the trauma team felt confident that Maddie was ready for the next step in her recovery.

The discharge papers were coordinated, and the lengthy reports of her care were forwarded to Children's Hospital. Jamie and I couldn't help but delight in the transfer. This meant she was definitely getting better. Doctors didn't say anything in regard to her prognosis, only that they had done all they could for her at the trauma center. A part of me ignored their words and grasped the memory of her opened eyes to power me through.

Maddie's transfer was a complicated and expensive undertaking. The intubation tube and breathing pump needed to remain uninterrupted during the switch from electric to battery. All her other tubes and wires had to stay intact. A small team from Children's Hospital was assembled to transfer her and there wasn't any room for me in the ambulance. Brandi offered to take us for the five-mile ride. Jamie sat up front and I slid into the back. The change in environment freed our minds and Jamie checked his phone.

"Jamie Lynn, you're not going to believe this—but I have a recording of everything." At first, I didn't understand. Jamie had dropped his phone in his quick response to Maddie's accident, and it had landed facedown with the video camera still recording. He tapped play. It was haunting. It started with the sound of running followed by primal screams of horror. Alone in the back seat, I started to tremble and quickly pleaded with him to turn it off. I finally got ahold of myself, but only because we had to go inside and attend to Maddie.

The new team was assembled in the ICU at Children's Hospital to discuss the next phase of Maddie's treatment. Recovery—the word was like an answered prayer. The natural course was to determine what was going on with her as a result of the trauma. They asked a lot of questions about the accident. One of the physicians inquired about the amount of time she was under water. Jamie pulled out his phone. He studied the screen. Astonished, he said, "Minimally, six and a half minutes."

Over the next day, the team conducted a number of tests to help determine her brain function. Nothing seemed to be wrong, and the doctors decided to reduce the strength of the breathing pump to get Maddie breathing on her own. The process, which occurred over days, was difficult to watch. Periodically, Maddie would thrash and try to pull every tube and wire from her body. She would tire and then the whole thing would start again. The sedative medications were eliminated. We were constantly in motion to keep her from pulling at the equipment. When we told her to leave her IVs in, she would listen, but then forget. Then she tugged at them and the whole process would start again. The struggle and the noises she made were awful. It was killing me to watch her suffer and each episode reminded me of the prayers and wishes I'd made.

Maddie's throat was sore, and making sounds, let alone speaking, was a challenge. But when she did speak, her words were strange and nonsensical. Once she fully regained her voice, she blabbered nonstop for hours. She sounded like someone else; her tone and manner were completely different from her own as she described horses and a man with a tall hat. Maddie's short-term memory loss had me repeatedly answering the question, "Why am I here?" every few minutes.

The doctor returned to check on Maddie and get an idea of how things were progressing.

"How's it going, Maddie?"

She replied with a belligerent tone.

The doctor glanced around the room at everyone assembled. He pointed to each person and asked her if she recognized them. He then pointed to me and asked again, "Do you know who this is, Maddie?"

"That's Carrie Underwood. But she kinda looks like my momma in those clothes."

I was stunned into a wretched silence and pasted a smile on my face. As soon as I could escape to the bathroom, I closed the door and cried heaving sobs of sadness. *My baby doesn't know me.* I cried some more but then recalled my prayers. *I'll take her any way I can get her.* With a deep sigh, I repeated, "I'll take her even if she doesn't know me." I went back to her bedside and tried to move on. The nurses were doing their best to reassure me that it was still too early to know the extent of her memory loss and that it could be only temporary. My relief was tear inducing when later in the day Maddie nonchalantly said, "Momma," as if she never forgot who I was.

Maddie's behavior continued to be erratic for hours. She was constantly trying to pull everything off—her IV lines, electrode stickers, and tape. She couldn't remember one minute to the next. We would start a DVD she selected and seconds later she'd demand we turn it off. She'd agree to leave the IVs in and moments later she tugged to yank them out. This continued for long hours into the evening and though it tried our patience, Jamie and I welcomed the task.

But then, hours turned into days. Maddie hadn't been able to sleep for the past two days, and we hadn't in longer than three. Maddie was moody and temperamental. And truthfully, as the hours passed and she continued to tear at her wires, I started to go a little crazy myself. Sometimes I'd catch her staring at me with a faraway look in her eyes. At the next check, Brandi was standing at the end of Maddie's bed as I begged them to give her something to sleep. They replied kindly, "We can't. We need to establish a baseline for her function. Medications will interfere with the process." Maddie looked right at Brandi and mouthed, "Get me out of here!"

We were late into the fourth night and Maddie still wasn't sleeping. I couldn't bring myself to leave her for any amount of time and the exhaustion was setting in. I stomped out to the on-duty nurse to fuss about Maddie's sleeplessness and irritability, ignoring my own fatigue. "Listen to me. I need you to help my little girl sleep!

She's past the point of exhaustion and between the constant check on vitals and those damn machines going off—sleep is impossible! PLEASE. DO. SOMETHING!"

Jamie had the patience of a saint and recognized I was starting to experience my own type of sleep psychosis. He and Casper pleaded with me to go take a shower and a nap. "You've got to take care of you, Jamie Lynn."

I relented and took a much-needed break. I knew they would take care of her.

Jamie lay with Maddie throughout the night, and they talked about all kinds of things. She still couldn't remember stuff for very long and asked the same questions repeatedly. But Jamie's calm soothed her. Sometime the following morning, Maddie finally fell asleep. When I woke up to find her sleeping peacefully, part of my anxiety was alleviated. Seeing her so comfortable was one of the most beautiful sights I had ever seen.

At 8:00 a.m. it was time for a staff shift change. The movement about the room woke Maddie. When she looked over at me, she nonchalantly asked, "Hey, Momma. Why am I here?" This time when I explained, she was able to remember. A few minutes later she said, "Hey, Momma? You going to give me that baby now?" Tears filled my eyes and I held her to me.

Maddie was a bit of a Ten Second Tom, a character from one of my favorite Drew Barrymore films, *50 First Dates*. Maddie would ask or say something, forget it instantaneously, and repeat herself moments later. The team announced we could move out of the

ICU. We were all beaming with happiness, despite Maddie's memory issues. With each hour, Maddie continued to improve, and she was able to sleep. Once in a while she asked again why she was in the hospital, but it wasn't as frequent as before. She began drinking fluids and loved going via wheelchair to the kitchen area for the Popsicles she couldn't get enough of. Moving and seeing her happy had us going back and forth for Popsicles several times a day. After the fourth trip, Maddie vomited. We panicked and called for the nurse, who explained that what happened was perfectly normal after not eating for days and the trauma Maddie had suffered. She suggested slowing down on the Popsicles to give her digestive tract a chance to recover. Jamie and I simultaneously exhaled in relief.

Within thirty-six hours of moving to the large hospital room, we received astonishing news. Maddie's doctor looked her over, flipped through the chart, and unceremoniously said, "I think you are ready to go home tomorrow." My immediate thought was, *What? How can that be?*

"We've done all we can do for her here. Her vitals are stable. She hasn't suffered a visible brain injury, and besides some memory issues, which I presume will resolve over time, she's good to go."

At first, I was shocked and, honestly, a little nervous too. He explained about potential therapies and follow-up appointments. As he spoke, I felt my confidence rise and realized with joy that we would be just fine. Our friend Giuseppe had been working behind the scenes making sure the waiting room always had food and drinks. He went to Target and bought Maddie clothes to wear home from the hospital. His attention to detail was impressive, and Maddie had everything she could possibly need. I helped Maddie take a shower, and it was then that I got a good look at her shrunken, weary body. Remarkably, she barely had a scratch anywhere except for her IV sites—such minor wounds for such a horrendous event.

The word spread to family and friends about Maddie's release. Everyone, including the physicians, agreed Maddie's recovery was miraculous. There was no other word for it. Five days after almost losing my daughter, we prayed in gratitude, thanked the staff, and drove the forty-five minutes home.

When I remember the events of February 2017, I first give thanks to God for returning Maddie to us. I learned the power of prayers and that miracles actually happen. The extensive support of friends, family, and medical professionals, coupled with faith, provided everything we needed to manage in such a traumatic time. At first, I focused on Maddie and her recovery. For the first several weeks, we had to stay vigilant about her taking her antibiotics and building up her strength. Maddie was at a high risk of developing pneumonia. Doctors were surprised she didn't develop the infection while in the hospital.

Maddie received stacks of cards from classmates and friends. A mass was dedicated to her at church and people for miles around prayed for her safety and well-being. The power of faith and prayers were ever present during her ordeal and we could feel the love all around us. Friends and strangers came together in coordinated efforts to see that not only our needs were met, but that those of our family were met as well. Sheriff Edwards—brother to the governor—and his family, Brandi, Diane, and Giuseppe, who came to the hospital daily, served vital roles helping us manage. Our families, including Casper, were selfless and giving. They took action and prayed along with everyone in our community. I feel like together, we willed Maddie back to us.

When her health started to stabilize, I became obsessed with speaking to and thanking the first responders who acted so heroically and saved critical moments that made all the difference in Maddie's outcome. Through Brandi's father I was able to get the names of the EMTs and reach out to everyone who helped us.

Once Maddie made a full recovery, I felt it was time to speak with her heroes. I thanked them profusely, knowing my words would never convey the extent of my gratitude. For Maddie's birthday, I invited the EMTs, John and Victoria, to the celebration, and I had a chance to talk to them. I wanted to understand as much as I could about that day. It was my way of processing the trauma and making sense of a miracle. When they arrived, it was difficult to see them in this environment. Memories flooded my brain, but instead I focused on John and Victoria. John looked exactly as I would expect a first responder to look. He's a good-sized man but possesses a sweetness too. Victoria, who comes off so casual yet capable, was warm and easy to be around. They were Maddie's very own guardian angels, and in turn, mine and Jamie's too.

"John, can you tell what you remember?" I asked.

"I had to make critical decisions in milliseconds," John said. "She was nonresponsive, and CPR wasn't working. I picked her up and ran while pounding on her back in case she had something lodged in her airway—which she didn't."

I asked questions, eager to learn the details of that day. "Did you use the paddles? A defibrillator?"

"No. We ran an IV line and I instinctively intubated her, knowing she needed oxygen. For a moment I didn't know if she'd make it. I may have skipped a couple steps—but I did what I thought was right at the moment."

It was only in talking to the EMTs that I learned the specifics of Maddie's coordinated rescue and all of the freakishly fortunate elements that came together to help her survive. I learned on weekdays, EMTs are situated at different exits on the interstate. On February 5, they happened to be stationed off exit 53, one mile from my in-laws' home. Because Holly had called 911 immediately, within eight minutes of the accident, the ambulance was on-site. If they had been anywhere else, the outcome would have been very different. But John and Victoria's quick response and rapid decision making was just the first of many elements that saved Maddie's life. On the way to the hospital, they radioed in the situation, warning the team at the hospital about the severity of the drowning and timing. A medical transport helicopter, AirLife, was activated and already at the hospital when Maddie arrived. By the time Jamie and I pulled up to the emergency room, the helicopter was en route to New Orleans.

Months later, at Maddie's honor roll assembly, a man approached me, and I learned he had piloted the helicopter that took Maddie to the trauma center. He'd heard the age, description, and location of the accident over the radio, and realized the injured girl was the same age as his own daughter, Madison, and they were in the same grade at the same school. He said, "I spent the entire flight praying for your daughter. I felt connected to her, knowing she and my daughter are the same age." Maddie joined our conversation, and he gifted her with a pair of AirLife wings that to this day she keeps displayed in her room.

Miracles were all around her from start to finish. I learned of several other key factors in Maddie's survival months later. A large rainfall had occurred the night before the accident, followed by an unseasonably cold day. The air and water temperatures, which were well below the normal range, played a key role in Maddie's recovery. Unusually cold temperatures inhibit bacteria growth, and this explains why she never developed a lung or bodily infection. The low temperature helped Maddie as she lost consciousness and stopped breathing. The cold may have helped prevent damage to her brain.

The truth remains, every factor—time, temperature, first responders, and Maddie's own body—came together in perfect synchronicity to bring her back to us. Me? I still think God played a huge role in coordinating the elements that saved her life. That and the thousands of prayers to bring her back to us.

The experience of almost losing Maddie compelled me to take

inventory of my own life and reprioritize. I pride myself on being a good mom. One who puts the needs of my daughter first and focuses on my family. But in the few years leading up to the accident, I had become engrossed in becoming a well-regarded performer and singer. I yearned to be the best at what I was doing and show Maddie that I could be the best mom, wife, and performer. What Maddie's accident helped me learn pretty quickly was that professional acceptance and esteem were superficial pursuits. I was reminded that our lives are truly a fragile gift, and I needed to flip my priorities.

But I didn't discover this on my own. Jamie is Catholic and Maddie attends a Catholic school, and after the accident, I made a commitment to myself and God, and backed it up by officially converting to Catholicism. The timing was perfect for me, as I had just discovered I was pregnant. In some ways I felt like I had to pay penance to show my gratitude. Father Mark, who had been with us during Maddie's ordeal, was the program's instructor. I dedicated myself to the three periods and four steps of RCIA, the Rite of Christian Initiation of Adults, which is a multistep process where you study the sacraments of Catholicism. Several people start the process and only a few make it all the way through to Baptism, Eucharist, and Confirmation. It took almost a year to complete, and I felt compelled by the blessings I received and my devotion to my faith to follow through with the program. The curriculum challenged us to think about our beliefs and the events that shaped who we are. The workshops gave me a chance to share Maddie's story, and more often than not, people found it difficult to assign reason to her outcome. Faith and prayer have always played a huge role in my life. Science and medicine helped save her, but I believe it was more than that.

As I got deeper into the program, I came to fully embrace my faith, and I began to understand I have no control and I need to put my trust in God. Those aren't just words to me. I walk the walk. This wasn't an epiphany or an "aha" moment. My change in perspective happened over time. I can't pinpoint the exact moment when I felt it; it was a feeling that grew within me, and it began to permeate my thoughts and approach to life. RCIA is rigorous and long. Many people drop out before the end, which is a pity because the more work you do, the greater the result. The shift in perspective ran so much deeper than I expected it to. By relinquishing that need to have control, I noticed that my anxiety level plummeted, and I was able to function free of medicinal interventions. That's not to say I don't have the occasional panic attack or moment of anxiety. I just resolve them differently.

My confidence grew, and for the first time in my life I felt an inner peace that far surpassed any sense of safety I had previously experienced. It gave new meaning to my existence. For those who are reading this and thinking, *Seriously?*, let me explain. My faith helped me realign my priorities. I was able to discard petty grievances and long-held fears about being good enough. It was freeing. My focus became my family, who always come first. I also developed a strong praying practice. I attend church almost every

Sunday, no matter where I am in the world, and I pray not just for me, but for others too. I pray for all the prayers that were gifted to Maddie. My devotion sets an example for my children. We need to believe in something bigger than ourselves, and our significance is rooted in our purpose. My purpose is to simplify and abandon the meaningless pressure of perfectionism and live in a manner that feels authentic to me. My previous insecurities, the ones that related to how successful I became professionally or recognition for my work, faded away. I understood that living authentically, from the heart and with integrity, provided the peace I had been without for so long.

Jamie and I made good on our promise to Maddie. All of us experienced overwhelming joy when we learned I was pregnant. I'd never seen Maddie smile so wide or felt Jamie's love more. I fulfilled my end of the bargain to God, and we welcomed baby Ivey into the family the following April. Ivey owned us from the moment she arrived. She has an infectious nature and is energetic. Every Spears says she is a mini-me. Momma is always saying, "She's exactly like you were when you were a toddler, Jamie Lynn." Ivey's birth reinforced the lessons I had learned in church and bolstered my faith in God. Her existence added a profound strength to our family's loving bond.

CHAPTER 11

A Good Mom

Even before I had ever considered getting pregnant, I had definite ideas of how I wanted my children to be raised. My children would have stability and constancy. As I mentioned earlier, I wanted to shield them from the type of chaos my parents' relationship wrought on me and my siblings. I can't deny that if the attempts I'd made to build a family with Casper had succeeded, I may have ended up just as I had started. Fortunately, I had learned enough in my young life to recognize the discord between us would lead down an unhealthy path. I knew going at parenting alone was preferable to staying with him. For a while, I believed it was going to be just Maddie and me. If I remained a single parent—so be it. But as the first years unfolded, I started to think about what bringing a man into my world would look like. I knew they would have to understand the guidelines I now used to govern my life. I refuse to fall victim to or expose my children to anyone who may be susceptible to addictive and abusive behaviors similar to the ones Casper exhibited. In the early days of my growing friendship with Jamie, I couldn't trust myself to recognize danger signs. There weren't any with Jamie, but I still lacked the confidence to trust my instincts. Reconnecting with my intuitive voice took time, and with someone like Jamie, who has well-defined principles for himself, that came easier than I expected. Discovering what works in my own life is the inverse of telling a lie. Momma taught me early on that once you lie, you need to tell a whole bunch of other lies to cover the first one. Making good decisions in my life works similarly. Once I made a healthy choice, it became easier to keep making them. I learned that balance, stability, and continuity are key elements to my well-being, and Jamie shared those ideals with me. Common beliefs became our foundation, and falling in love was a gentle slide for both of us.

As a result of my upbringing, I manage my life in a precise and exacting way. I'm a scheduler and calendar keeper. I make lists and charts, color-coded and alphabetized. My work requires a lot of travel and time on set when I can't use my phone. During filming no one is permitted to use a cell phone because producers are concerned that pictures, recordings, or information will get leaked and tip viewers off on the show's plot twists or expose behind-the-scenes material. To make things easier for all of us, I made small notebooks of information that Jamie and the girls can refer to anytime. We keep an extensive detailed weekly calendar for the entire family, so we know where everyone is at any given moment. I make sure to include pickup times and carpool drivers' names. Phone numbers are listed for professionals and friends. There is a small book for medications and dosages. Can you see that I have a tendency to plan for all eventualities? My husband will tell you that I am a functioning obsessive-compulsive. He's right. After Maddie's birth, I realized that scheduling and consistency brought me peace of mind. Not only did I want to make sure she had everything she needed, but I never wanted to forget a thing.

Now, years later, with a husband and two daughters, I've had to expand and develop effective ways to stay on top of things. My creative mind enjoys putting these scheduling tools together for my family, and it makes things easier for all of us. It's the residual effects of growing up in a chaotic home where schedules were changed often, and stability came in spurts. The need to feel like I have control over my time and environment is essential to my well-being. The operative words are "feel like," because if life has taught me anything, it's that we have very little control over anything. We possess our thoughts, actions, and reactions. Beyond that, it's in God's hands.

I'm only a part-time control freak. Spontaneity gives me a chance to join my daughters in whatever they are doing. I try to remember to be grateful and appreciate the small moments. My definition of being a good mom is rooted in my own experience. I believe that everyone's concept of being a good mom is different and varies depending upon how they were reared. From the onset I knew my children would come before the needs of anyone else in my life. I always wanted them to feel not just valued or wanted, but secure in knowing they were my priority. For Maddie, it was especially important because of her experiences with her dad. Casper did what he could to be a father to Maddie, but as the early years passed, he disappeared more and more. He was supportive after her accident and during her recovery, but soon he vanished for long periods of time.

By the time Maddie turned nine, Casper had once again succumbed to using. Maddie started to talk about changing her last name to Watson. Her determination bordered on demand. We explained she didn't understand the lengthy process of adoption and that changing her name meant that she would give up the name Aldridge for the rest of her life. She insisted she did in fact understand, and it was important to her that she share our name. Casper wasn't having visitations with her anymore, and as his run-ins with the law continued, I knew things had to change. I spent months contemplating what was best for Maddie and everyone else— including Casper's parents. I wanted desperately for Maddie to have a relationship with them, but the rift between father and daughter made a connection with her biological grandparents difficult. I spoke in length about this with Jamie, my folks, and even my priest.

I wanted to do the right thing, but most importantly, Maddie's well-being had to be considered above all else. I shared my deepest fears with Jamie—how I hated playing God and making such a profound decision that would affect Maddie forever. Jamie had always been supportive of Casper remaining Maddie's father in name and deed and stood by as Casper slowly disappeared from her life.

As I wrote earlier, Maddie and Jamie's relationship is undeniably special. In the years since he joined our duo, he has been a father figure to her, and their connection has only deepened. She shows him well-deserved respect not just as my husband, but as a father. He had taken on the responsibility of fatherhood for several years and at times that role can be difficult. In the beginning of our marriage, I had a hard time relinquishing responsibility over Maddie's care. I had been her sole provider for so long, and changing that dynamic was challenging for me. Slowly, over time, Jamie earned my trust and proved he was invested in Maddie's well-being. That faith allowed me to share my load and bring him into all aspects of her life. Once we considered all the factors, Jamie and I chose to push for adoption.

We spoke several times with Casper, who at first felt like we were pushing him out of her life. Eventually I was able to convince him I was speaking for Maddie. She wanted to share our family name and feel connected to us. It took a few weeks for Casper to relent. After Maddie's initial interviews with mediators, Casper felt, if not good, at least satisfied Maddie would be happier this way. The process took months and coincided with the arrival of Ivey Joan.

We encouraged Casper to remain in all our lives. Sadly, as months passed, he found himself in legal trouble again and again, and he disappeared once more.

Unlike Maddie's chaotic arrival in the world, Ivey's was more typical. There wasn't any press or media. In the ten years since I gave birth the first time, social media had emerged, and that platform gave us control over what was released to the public. We had the power in our hands to share what we were comfortable sharing with the world. No one would have knowledge or pictures before we did. I could crop and enhance the pictures to display the parts of the experience that felt right to share. No one would twist or manipulate what came directly from me. Jamie and I drove to the hospital late. In the evening, Momma and Daddy stayed with Maddie, who was given special privileges to stay up late and miss school for the arrival of her baby sister. She laid out a special set of "big sister scrubs" to wear the next day, and she could barely contain herself.

The nurse assigned to me was phenomenal. She made everything easier. I was completely laid-back, while Jamie's frenetic movements and discomfort were comical. You'd think he was the one giving birth. He was so stoic and strong during Maddie's hospitalization that it never occurred to me he'd be uneasy during my delivery. Jamie hates to see me or anyone he loves suffer in any way. Unfortunately, for all fathers sharing in the experience, the birth process can be a painful event, especially when the epidural is administered only after contractions begin. The morning progressed without complications and Momma appeared to share in the experience. While Jamie held my hand and stared at the opposite wall to try and stay upright, Ivey arrived, fulfilling so many dreams. Maddie walked into the room glowing with joy. The four of us were encased in love and awed by one another.

Becoming a mother of two happens instantaneously. The adjustment happens in real time, and for me the adjustment was easier than the months of pregnancy that had ravaged my body. I learned something about myself during my pregnancy with Ivey that I'd had no time to consider during Maddie's: I hated being pregnant. I'm endlessly grateful for a baby—and a healthy one at that. But the actual pregnancy? To this day, I'm not really sure why but I develop a type of prenatal depression, spending months exhausted, listless, and in physical pain. Difficulty breathing makes me miserable and not easy to be around. Astonishingly, within hours of delivering, I hit a level of unprecedented euphoria. The relief of the symptoms combined with the baby's healthy arrival is enough to ease the problem—I imagine there's a hormonal component too.

As reality set in and Jamie and I became parents of two girls, acclimating to our new normal worked out better than I anticipated. Ivey took to breastfeeding like it was a competitive sport. The second time around revived my love of connecting with my baby in this manner and providing nutrition in this special way. She latched easily and only stopped because she started to ask for my boob in full sentences.

Like Britney and me, Maddie and Ivey are just under ten years apart. It's a bit surreal watching them interact. Sometimes I observe them and get caught up in my own memories. When Ivey was first born, Maddie wanted to do everything for Ivey. I had to explain that there are some things that only a momma can do. In the months that followed, Maddie had to adjust to sharing me with her sister. This wasn't as difficult for me because I had plenty of Ivey time while Maddie was at school. But Maddie, she struggled with this concept. I told her, "Maddie. You had me all to yourself for a long time. Ivey needs to get some of my time. Remember, none of my babies will ever get me all to themselves." That seemed to pacify her and eventually we all adapted to our new life. After the adoption and Ivey's birth, our family felt whole, like the pieces of a puzzle fit together. Don't get me wrong, there may be a few more pieces added down the road, but for now things just feel right.

For me, being a good mom means making hard choices and establishing limits. Limits remind kids they are safe and loved. I've learned through action and observation that children and teens will push through boundaries and try to take control before they are old enough to know the consequences. It bears repeating that I don't want my girls to pay for my mistakes, but I also need to give them time to be children, vulnerable in a world that can be both permissive and severe. I grew up too fast, and I often remind Maddie to take her time and enjoy being young. Time goes by so quickly without us wishing it away. As an adult I can finally see that for the truth it is. Moments are all we have and to live in as many as possible is the gift. It's why I try to be spontaneous and keep life at home uncomplicated. Whenever possible, work is something I strive to keep separate from my family time. The thing about me is that I'm not a fancy girl. I play dress-up for a living, but I prefer oversized T-shirts and comfortable shorts. I'm a slides and sneakers kind of girl. My face is typically free of makeup and my hair is either tied up or under a hat. I'm no-frills. I think part of the reason I don't fuss about my appearance daily is because I want my girls to see me as Momma, not a character. Time is precious and I hate wasting it applying makeup. Unless I'm playing dress-up with Ivey, which can happen at any time of day.

I constantly work at being a good mom to Maddie and Ivey. It means I have to show up every day—sometimes that means via FaceTime or a phone call. Ivey is still so young that she requires time, just like any toddler soaking up the world and learning by experience. With Maddie, she's approaching on the years when she'd be mortified to read about herself in this book. But it doesn't keep me from being her softball mom who does everything possible to watch every single game—even if it's via the internet. I show up for her by being available whenever she needs me and encouraging her to be comfortable in her own skin. I always have her back and love her unconditionally—not for what she does but simply because she's mine. Okay—and Jamie's too.

The right partner makes being a good parent possible. Historically I feel like I am terrible in relationships. The truth: Until you're in the right relationship, it's impossible to be a good partner. I'll be the first one to tell you I'm not perfect. In fact, some days I'm a terrible wife. Most of the time I am loving and supportive as I can be. And Jamie gets me. He understands my quirks and convictions and loves me anyway. Our parenting style is firm, loving, and infused with humor. Ivey's too young to comment but I think Maddie would tell you we can be demanding at times but come at it with love and respect. For the most part, we would say the same of her. Well, except when she's testing her new teenage limits!

Like all moms, I do need my own space. There isn't a whole lot of downtime in my life, just by nature of who I am. I need to have purpose in just about everything I do. But I do have a few guilty pleasures. After Jamie and the girls are asleep, I love mindless reality television, like *The Real Housewives*. Late at night you can usually find me staring, mouth agape, at something one of the wives has said while I fold a giant load of laundry. Remember, purpose? I also love to read scripts. I love to immerse myself in the world someone has visualized for the screen. When I can't find time to myself, I find great pleasure in a fizzy bottle of Coca-Cola. But just a little. I'm trying to set a good example!

As a family, we stay strong by showing up for each other every day, loving uncontrollably, and avoid driving each other crazy. At the core of it, I work at being a good mom. It's not something you perfect. Sometimes I've got the plan and other times I close my eyes and jump. I've got a safe place to land. Jamie's my steadfast Louisiana man, and together with our girls, we built a beautiful family.

CHAPTER 12

You Can Take the Girl Out of Louisiana

My views about the way I live my life today are the same as when I played Zoey. As a young performer, the girl who fulfilled a dream and became a star, I grabbed and maximized every opportunity that came my way. The teenage me envisioned a future that included acting and singing. When I closed my eyes and pictured my future, visions of the performer I wanted to become appeared. Realizing any dream requires the willingness to suffer, learn, and endure painful experiences that ultimately change a person in fundamental ways; or so that's what I've been told. For me, taking my journey from child star to teen mom, to adult performer and wife, has brought me full circle to what fundamentally makes me happy.

Early on, I made a promise to myself: I will do everything in my power to create a stable and happy environment for my family. The needs of my children will always preempt my own until they are capable of doing that for themselves. Years before I became a mother, Daddy's lengthy drinking and the realization of the utter pain and shame I'd experienced in my childhood, coupled with Momma's incessant need to convince the world that everything was fine, became the impetus for that pledge to myself. Becoming Maddie's mother reinforced that truth. I never fathomed anyone or anything would derail me from keeping that promise. If I'm anything, I'm strong and resolute about commitments to myself and others. Then, how did I get so far off course for a while there?

The decision to have Maddie and the decision to try to build a life with Casper were both instinctive and logical. My intuition has always been a powerful force for me. Once I discovered I was pregnant, there wasn't a moment where I genuinely considered not having her. Everyone else had their doubts. For me and my teenage heart, she was a gift. In the beginning, I truly believed Casper and I would mend our hurts to create a family. Love, especially young love, is a powerful force that blinded me to not just logic, but my gut instincts too. The mistake I made over and over again in Maddie's first few years by allowing Casper's behaviors—so similar to my father's—to go unchecked left me utterly disgusted with myself. It took years for me to work through those feelings and only strengthened my resolve to prevent that type of abusive behavior from affecting my children in the future.

The promise to them starts with me. I learned how to take care of myself. Workouts, which historically were designed to keep me lean and fit, loaded with cardio, were replaced with a more dynamic approach to fitness incorporating strength of body and mind. My trainer-turned-friend Julie Day taught me to look at food, my body, and my spirituality in a more holistic manner. This helped me have a healthy relationship with my own mind and body. But like everyone else, when the alarm goes off in the morning, I lie still, staring up at the ceiling, and wonder, *What if I didn't go today?* At first, staying curled up in my bed is tempting. Then I think about the fallout of not taking care of my needs. My fitness routine fortifies my body, but more, it helps me manage my stressors and emotions. I've also made a vow to talk through my anxiety and fears. It's my form of therapy. And I pray, a lot. These practices are only part of how I preserve this commitment. The other piece is more complicated. I had to relearn how to trust my judgment. The relationship I had with Casper was inundated with the same codependent behaviors that my parents exhibited as a result of my daddy's issues. Fear and negativity kept Casper in my life for much too long. For a while, my childhood experiences infused my relationship, and I almost started to believe I was doomed to repeat the mistakes of my parents. That's one part of my Louisiana life I had no interest in retaining.

My career and the resulting emotional journey, which took me far from Louisiana to California and beyond, led me back to my roots. The experiences that were so vital to learning what works for me reinforced how much I adore the simplicity and quiet of a Louisiana lifestyle.

I knew early in my career that I had very little interest in living in LA. I never took to the vibe or the fast-paced energy of the city. Don't get me wrong, I can keep up, but the vapid nature of Hollywood never felt like home to me. I love working there, and I appreciate the passion industry professionals put into everything they do. Watching a project come together is, quite frankly, amazing. A myriad of things happens between a script being optioned to appearing on the screen. I'm invigorated by taking part in the process of creating characters and bringing stories to the world.

Whether for the small screen or a major motion picture, in Hollywood or on location, I dedicate myself 100 percent to my job and become immersed wherever I'm temporarily living. I explore each place and try to make it mine while I'm living there. I get out and run to get a feel for the landscape and discover places I'd like to visit. I typically move about unrecognized thanks to my tendency to dress down. Much of the time I'm with my daughters, so caught up in them, I don't bother to think about being seen. One of the ways I manage long shoots is by having my family with me as much as possible. Our girls travel with me or visit on weekends. I make frequent trips home too. Maddie has a full schedule. I respect her time and appreciate whenever she can join me on location. Their support is invaluable and keeps me balanced when I'm far from home. The transient nature of being an actor can leave me feeling untethered and disconnected. I've learned that having the people I love around me nurtures me and allows me to be a mother, wife, and performer.

My profession lets me have new experiences—from taking on characters to spending time in various locations—but, when it's done, I return home to Louisiana. Home is both the place I love and the family around me. It's where I abandon my persona, cast aside my characters, and ground myself in the stability of the life I've built. When I return to Hammond, I cling to the ease and predictability of the everyday. It's where I become Jamie Lynn, wife and mother. Both sides of my life are equally challenging, but my family keeps me incredibly humble and rooted in a way performing simply cannot.

As an adult, I've realized that my Louisiana ways, the things I love most about life in the South, are within me. Momma and Daddy instilled in me a set of Southern values that are ingrained into who I've become as an adult. The South gives me a sense of warmth that's different from people from other parts of the country. It's not better or worse, just mine. I was raised to respect and give deference to my elders—you earn respect by giving it. Manners are important. In my career, I did everything I could not to abandon my moral compass. Despite the mistakes along the way, I owned up to each one and tried to move in the right direction. In the entertainment world it can be easy to get off course, especially if you lose your integrity. The more famous you become, the easier it is to lose those parts of yourself. For me, I try my best to nurture my strong moral code, embrace faith, and surround myself with like-minded people. Living in Louisiana helps to reinforce these principles for me.

Everyone carries a piece of where they come from. I certainly do. The work I do varies in scope and size. For something as small as an interview, I am determined to convey my thoughts and responses in a manner that reflects the essence of who I am. At this point, I've become comfortable being me and I want that to show. It's taken me years and a few missteps to get to this point and to regain my confidence. I've made mistakes and paid for them. Sometimes I'd start a project and realize it's no good; I paid for those with more than money. Other times someone else makes the mistakes and they pay. I've turned down lots of jobs that were lucrative and may have propelled my career. I never do anything that doesn't feel right. Don't get me wrong, there are some meetings I take wondering if I really want that specific job. But that's the beauty of the entertainment industry; sometimes you show up expecting it to end with an offer for a role, and over the course of the meeting, it leads you to a completely different outcome and offer. Some executives who have seen my work tend to assume they know me. After we meet, their level of expectation is changed, and new opportunities come my way. This was the case when I learned about the Netflix drama *Sweet Magnolias*. After Ivey was born, I was interested in pairing with a team on a music/film project called *Roots*. Songwriting, which is basically storytelling set to music, reminded me how much I adore being a part of the visual medium. I started to think about how I could infuse one with the other. The music was complete, but to develop the concept I envisioned, which grew out of the changes in my life since Maddie's accident, I needed a creative team. I went out to LA to meet with executives from Netflix and Hulu. I met with two executives from Netflix, who were amiable, and we found ourselves talking about a myriad of topics. And just like in a movie, one of the women asked if I was interested in acting again. I said, "Yes. I'd love to. I'm ready to get back to work." She went on to explain that within weeks a new show was going into production, and I would be perfect for one of the roles—but not a lead role, and I'd have to read for the part. It was a great way to get back into a series. Immediately they sent me "sides" and I loved the character. Within a day, I got a call that told me the production team was leaving for Atlanta the following day and if I was truly interested, I needed to meet them for breakfast that morning. I met the executive producers at the Four Seasons, and I immediately felt like this was right for me. "We still need you to read, Jamie Lynn. But we feel pretty good. Oh, and we start in Atlanta in three weeks. Will that work?" The timing and circumstance couldn't have been better. God was definitely working the strings.

I think one of the things that surprises people about me the most is the dichotomy of my personality. I can be very serious, intense, and introspective. The flip side of that is that I am blunt, funny, and approachable. I recently did a photo shoot. If you've ever done any type of photo shoot, then you know the glam that appears on the page takes hours to attain. I don't always have the same team to help enhance my appearance, so I make it a point to put everyone at ease as soon as we get there. The people behind the scenes—wardrobe, makeup, and hair—are the real geniuses. Print shoots are different from film. Photos require a number of looks that provide snapshots of me appearing as myself. I infuse my personality and playfulness into the process. To achieve an authentic picture, I combine elements of acting into print work.

When I'm acquainted with a team, I feel relaxed and can get going with the stylist. They always come well prepared—some better than others. An array of clothes and accessories are laid out and we bring the concepts together. A good stylist sets up combinations; a great stylist is one who knows who they are dressing and brings a vision. Sometimes multiple people weigh in on a look. But the final call is always mine—remember the control thing? Don't let anyone tell you that makeup is just a mask. A makeup artist is a true professional. Quite frankly, they are remarkable at using shading and light to maximize a person's assets. I especially enjoy working with a makeup professional who truly makes me look like a pulled-together version of myself, rather than a doll.

With hair there is a completely different approach. The hair professionals work together to create a color and hairstyle vision. Each outfit gets its own hair and makeup change. I usually love what they pull together, but when I don't, adjustments are made. To be honest, I usually wait to see how things look on camera or computer screen before I interject.

While hair and makeup work in tandem with each other to transform me, I try to relax and often chat with the group. When I'm in the makeup chair, it's like sitting around with a bunch of people talking about everything from shoes to children and world events. Recently, I sat quietly as the subject of young Hollywood came up and someone mentioned a name. They laughed when I asked, "Who's that?" Someone said, "Come on, Jamie Lynn—you know who that is." I responded kindly by explaining that a full-time mom living in Louisiana has very little time for celebrity gossip. It reminds me how separate the two parts of my life really are and how much I appreciate that arrangement.

Growing up as a versatile performer and athlete, I got used to changing in front of others. It's a by-product of the job. In a professional situation, I do what needs to be done and there's no time for inhibitions. I've got to try on all different types of clothes and combinations to achieve a look. I know that each picture tells a story or highlights an aspect of my personality. Sometimes I look in the mirror and dislike what I'm wearing. But it's a look and it helps me become the version of myself we are all seeking to capture on film.

In preparation for the shooting portion of the day, I create an internal dialogue to get where I need to be mentally. I may approach the set feeling like my boobs are positioned wrong or my legs need to be tanner, but the shot needs to get done—and that's the job. Once the shutter is pressed, I assume the role that's intended for a given look. It's acting with expressions and body language.

When a team prepares me for a role, it's a distinct look for a character I bring to life. For me, the most peculiar aspect of this is dyeing my hair a completely different color. I usually have to do this several weeks in advance of a shoot, and looking at myself in a mirror can be unsettling. The effect can be so unlike something I'd choose for myself. But I remind myself it's temporary. The bonus to wearing a color long term is that slipping into character is much easier. For example, in a series shoot, I'm often in similar attire, and once the clothes and makeup are on, I can slide right into character. For a character like Noreen, who I play on *Sweet Magnolias*, I find portraying her inspiring. She is living a life not too dissimilar to my own experience. I feel like infusing her with a strong spirit is almost healing for me. She has to take charge of her life and prepare for a baby without the support of a husband or fiancé. Noreen and I have parallel life experiences. Sometimes when I'm filming, I smile to myself thinking, *Dang, she's got her shit way more together than I did.*

My history pervades every aspect of my performances. The pursuit of perfectionism and my commitment to professionalism is born of my upbringing. I practice my lines and refine my performance as needed. Dedication to my craft permeates everything I do, in order to cultivate a reputation as being both reliable and competent. I want to leave the set knowing that everyone sees me as a consummate professional. Within the parameters of all that, my integrity is paramount. I remain true to myself and to the characters I portray. I've got to be comfortable in whatever role I play to make it authentic. Fortunately, I can be comfortable in many different roles because of my love for creating characters. I can play an ingenue, even though that's not my personality, just like I can be the antagonist—especially one who is misunderstood. At heart I'm a storyteller. The medium doesn't really matter. If there's a good story to tell, with a character that has depth and purpose, I want to be a part of it. The beauty of becoming part of any story's journey is that ultimately it will lead me back to the stability of life with my family in Louisiana.

Writing and performing music allows me to share parts of myself and create stories based on my experiences. It also gives me an opportunity to explore my imagination and weave tales of life and love. Being a songwriter and performer ticks all the boxes for me—character building, storytelling, and performing. By default, so much of who I am and where I come from is woven into just about every song I've written. I think just about everyone is shocked when they discover the number of songs I have in my catalog. Of the over one hundred songs I am credited with, only a handful have been released as of this writing. I have written chart-topping hits for performers like Jana Kramer and received awards for my work. When the time is right, I plan to collaborate with other performers in the future and bring more of my songs to the public.

Timing has become an essential aspect of my life. I wear a lot of hats and want to ensure I'm fully present in that particular job. I spent years doing what others thought was best instead of what

I felt was right for me. For now, I'm enjoying being a mom, acting, and partnering with Jamie to achieve our respective goals. I'm proud of my roots and the life I've created with my family in Louisiana. I can't imagine living anywhere else, and sharing this part of myself with the world reaffirms my connection to everything I cherish. The journey from teen mom to who I am today, with its bumps, triumphs, and self-discovery, has convinced me that I've got to do something for myself, something that will serve my whole family. I want to create a life suffused with giving and authenticity.

CHAPTER 13

My Testimony

On June 23, 2021, my sister broke her silence in regard to the oppressive nature of her 2008 conservatorship. Throughout the weeks that followed, she had the media and internet world stage to speak freely—to share her truth. During a couple of her statements, she made sweeping allegations, using words like "my family" and "those who should have helped." At no point did my sister lift the veil on what or who is truly responsible for her challenges. By excluding this, she allowed an onslaught of hate that put me and my family at risk.

Her references to me left me reeling. I have only ever had her back. From the earliest days of Britney's challenges, I have protected her at every turn. Too young to know better, to understand that it's okay if you're not okay, I helped keep Britney's emotional episodes hidden from the world. It started early, when I was in my tweens, and I had to defuse rumors my classmates repeated, and I continued to protect her until just recently, when she decided I didn't need protecting and threw me to the proverbial media wolves.

Despite her comments, I still support what is best for her. I'm only saddened that in her current state of mind, she is incapable of supporting me in the same way. My siblings and I have been traumatized by the distorted vision my parents have of loyalty and success, the impact of exposure, and the flip side of fame. I'm not looking for pity. I want Britney and the world to know she isn't the only one who is left with the scars from our early years of delinquency and manipulation.

I am immensely grateful for my career and the events that have led me here, to the life I now enjoy. But that came from luck, hard work, and owning up to my mistakes along the way. My sister's diatribe assigns blame outward without any self-reflection.

I want to reiterate that my early childhood was good, despite the growing chaos in our home. But at that time, we weren't different from many other families. Everyone's attention, especially that of my sister, fed my later desire to garner her approval and acceptance. I'd do just about anything to stay in her good graces and allowed myself to be manipulated my entire life. Coaxed by my parents to be a version of myself that supported the family—that is, my sister's ever-expanding career—meant I was permitted to follow my own dreams as long as they were in line with hers. My aim was to try and be a good girl and that left me vulnerable to my parents' machinations. Oddly enough, when I unexpectedly became pregnant at sixteen, I discovered the ability to think and make decisions that were best for me, without seeking their approval.

As a mother, I can see how much a child yearns for their parents' approval. As I mentioned earlier, my sister was a mother figure to me, and maintaining our connection—to know she loved me—motivated me to do anything to keep her happy. I can look back with a new perspective, not exactly hindsight, and admit that pacifying my sister, keeping her needs met, and appeasing everyone along the way, only added fuel to a fire. The fire has grown into an inferno.

Early on, I believed that if I tried to let her know how worried I was for her well-being, I would also risk losing my sister's regard and love. Later, I was caught up in my own life, and my parents convinced me Britney was fine. Clearly, she wasn't. In recent years, and this past summer in particular, when my sister spoke to the world about her feelings regarding my parents' purposeful strategy to garner fame, Britney's impassioned statements included the wrongdoings of everyone involved, without any reference to herself.

Throughout the past few years, living through an unimaginable trauma with Maddie, I chose to make changes in my own life, and try to keep myself from being sucked into the drama in which my family is so notably involved. But it hasn't been easy.

From the time I was able to follow directions, I was instructed to be the most devoted sister. My parents didn't have to ask. I adored Britney from my earliest memories. It's usually the natural way of things. Devotion comes in many forms and mine is deep, abiding, and perpetual. At the age of seven, while I was learning what loyalty meant to my family, millions of kids my age were kneeling at the altar of Britney Spears. While I was behaving, clearing a path, staying out of trouble, stepping aside, and making sure I didn't cause my sister any distress, Britney's number of fans expanded exponentially. And no one was happier for her than me. I knew how hard she worked for it and all the things our family had sacrificed to support not only her dream, but mine too. But there were concessions, excuses, and perhaps too much tolerance. Early on, I just thought, *This is normal. It's how all families love and protect each other.* But there has never ever really been anything normal or ordinary about growing up a Spears. We've always been critiqued and evaluated by the world at large. Therein lies the rub. No one knows better than my sister how calculating the press can be. How everything she says is spun and revised to suit a purpose. In our world, words matter and should be used purposefully.

If I am guilty of anything, it's of enabling the situation to continue by not speaking up earlier in her career. I often wonder if I had, would it have made any difference? There are things I said to keep my family's name unsullied by gossip, and other things I should have said when I sensed something was amiss. I am now just coming to terms with how my family's philosophy of making everything appear fine and excusing Britney's behavior has led us to where we are today.

As a child, I realized early on that my sister's career usurped anything else in my family's life. I was young and didn't have a say in the matter. I love my life now, but from the age of seven until I was well into my teens, I often wished Britney would quit the industry and we could just go home to Louisiana. The demands of her career, and my parents' focus on her, left me feeling if not insignificant, then inconsequential for years. So much attention was devoted to Britney, to protecting their asset, that I was left to take care of myself at all turns. The only way I could do that was to try in vain to be the loyal, loving, and devoted Spears family member. No one protected me from the backlash of my older sister's struggles or prepared me for what our silence would cost. We were a tight-knit family torn apart by money, distorted truths, and undisclosed personal issues. Again, it's okay not to be okay. You can thank Piglet from *Winnie-the-Pooh* for those auspicious words.

I finally received the wake-up call I needed to change. During quarantine, when all of us were living under one roof again, I saw that same childhood dynamic with adult eyes. Britney became enraged about something trivial. She came at me screaming and getting up in my face while I was holding Ivey, who was only twenty-two months at the time. Despite my best efforts, Britney continued on the attack, and Maddie had to get in between us to protect her little sister until my parents could finally get Britney to retreat. The girls and I were visibly shaken. I decided then and there—*NO MORE!* Momma begged me not to upset my sister. "Jamie Lynn. Please don't upset your sister anymore; you know how she is. She can tell when you're anxious." I stood mouth agape. I couldn't believe she was asking me to put my feelings and those of my children aside to, once again, pacify my sister. Experiencing this dynamic as an adult and a mother was the catalyst I needed to remove myself from the situation. I wouldn't ask my children to pretend everything was fine to soothe my parents or sister, nor would I continue to do so myself. Although the pandemic necessitated that we stay together, I made certain that the girls and I distanced ourselves from that cycle of behaviors.

In my position as Britney's sister and the daughter of Jamie and Lynne Spears, I didn't want any part of the legalities established to protect her. However, a couple of years into the evolving conservatorship, when Britney established her will, she asked me to serve as the trustee for her two children only in the event that she would not be able to do so herself. This was separate from her team's request for me to reside as a trustee over her children's trust in the conservatorship. After several months and careful consideration, I decided to remove myself from that role, citing that the developing issues could potentially create a conflict. My role was to remain impartial and simply be a sister and aunt. I have never participated in the conservatorship as my sister's personal representative or her financial conservator. In essence, I have never made decisions for my sister. I was raised to be devoted, to protect my family, and to honor the privacy that all families are afforded. I was always there to help address any issues that she brought to me. And now, after her testimony, that creed has bit me on the ass, again. I have stood by and protected my sister to my own detriment and that of my husband and two daughters.

Since her testimony, I have been accused and convicted of everything from theft to neglect in the court of public opinion. Jamie, the girls, and I have been threatened. There are times I don't feel safe. I spent the greater part of my life trying to protect her even when it wasn't in my best interest, and I had hoped that her statements would clarify that I had no part in any of her issues. I've always tried my best to protect my sister, but now I have to put my two daughters' protection first.

There are thousands of people who have turned their adoration into judgments and bias based upon the media's snippets of incomplete information and speculation. In the court of public opinion, if you are a member of the Spears family, you are labeled detestable and reprehensible. I am guilty of loving my whole family and wanting what is best for all of them. I always have. But I've created my own family, which always comes first. And our last name is Watson.

In 2008, when the conservatorship was implemented, I was a seventeen-year-old girl with a new baby. My focus was single-mindedly on my daughter Maddie. From my perspective, I only knew my sister's behavior had changed drastically in the previous year. Remembering that period of my life brings up the loneliness I suffered by not having my sister there for me during the one time in my life I desperately needed her. Looking back, maybe I should have done more when I lived in California, but again, I was a child. Britney was the adult, and she had promised me she was fine. By accepting her declaration I enabled many of the behaviors that contributed to her downward spiral at that time. The world saw she was in crisis, and it appeared the conservatorship protected her at a time when she was in need.

And now? None of this has anything to do with me other than that Britney is my sister. I will continue to love and support her whether there is a conservatorship or not. I have no skin in this media spectacle other than dealing with the shrapnel her explosive testimony blasted my way, but that pales in comparison to the heartbreak in my older daughter's eyes as she hears the whispers amongst her peers. I know the truth. In a recent text from my sister, she stated herself: "I know it's not your fault and I'm sorry for being so angry at you. Although I'm your big sister, I need you more than you need me and always have." I pray for the day she shares these words with the world. I have no control over anything the media reports and cannot be held responsible for something I have absolutely no control over.

It took twenty-plus years for me to learn what healthy devotion and loyalty to family look like. I still feel that like every family, our family should be given the same consideration when dealing with personal issues and trauma. There's not a person alive who wants their struggles to be reported in the news, followed up with commentary and judgments from their own family. It's unfair to assume that Britney's fame excludes her from her right to privacy or that of her family. But privacy hasn't been afforded to any of us, and my parents' determination to keep Britney free from embarrassment and public humiliation may have come at a high cost that wasn't in her best interest.

There are no sides here, and there can be no winner. I love and support my sister. I believe that my sister and the medical professionals that she chooses can seek the healthiest outcome for her future. For some, this ordeal may have been about her music, her contribution to the industry, and the money. For me, this has only ever been about the girl who gave so much in pursuit of her dream to sing for millions. The flip side was everything Britney sacrificed along the way: her privacy, dignity, and overall health. When the cameras turn away and everyone's moved on to the next headline, I will still be here for my sister, no matter what is said or done between us.

I have immense gratitude for the blessings in my life. The people who love and support me make all the difference. I've trusted my instincts. Jamie and our daughters will continue to be my priority, as I am theirs. We've put in the work to build our life, and everything else, the chaos that surrounds us, will fade away at some point. My job is to protect the ones I love with honesty and vehemence. I have realized that without health and balance in my life, nothing else matters.

Life is a series of lessons that challenge us. My faith, tested and reaffirmed, ensures that I protect my family, offer unconditional love, and share the values I embrace—to lead a moral and good life.

I have learned not to enable, and as much as I want to, I can't help someone who doesn't want it. Devotion and trust are earned and, if we are lucky, reciprocated. I continue to learn as I go, and know I may have many challenges yet to endure. This all boils down to knowing who I am and living authentically. I must admit, though, a little more faith and a focus on our blessings may have made a difference in the past. I know it does now.

CHAPTER 14

Breaking the Cycle

Professionally, when people first meet me, they probably assume they already know my character. Early in my career I was taught to be what was expected for a job. Much of the time I spent in Nashville kept me in a cycle of being all the things people needed me to be. But near the end of that experience, I started to realize I can only work to please myself. The standard of perfectionism I had set for myself was predicated on someone else's vision. There wasn't any pleasure in that. Coming to terms with what really brought me pleasure and how to cultivate more joy in my life didn't happen until after Maddie's accident and my subsequent religious study.

Because of my upbringing, I learned early on about the

consequences of making emotional decisions; making choices based on how you feel about something will bite you on the ass every time. So often I remember watching Daddy walk out the door because he felt he needed to—that he couldn't cope without a drink. He didn't have the awareness to consider how his actions were affecting everyone around him. I believe the same is true of Momma, as she enabled behaviors that had huge ramifications for the family and her children's well-being. My brother, Bryan, often did the same, while Britney struggled to make healthy decisions that served herself or others. Inversely, I spent years doing things that felt wrong for me and right for everyone else. It was almost my undoing.

In the years since Maddie's miracle, I have truly experienced an awakening of sorts. I've shifted my perspective on how I live and make decisions on a daily basis. My philosophy is born of gratitude and a willingness to give. I try not to do one thing and feel another. The word "authentic" is what helps me stay strong in my conviction. In other words, I need to be true to the core. I want to be the same person whether someone is looking or not, which affords me internal accountability.

Life has given me so many precious blessings that my intention is to give them back. I know watching my child stop breathing and slip away changed me in a fundamental way. I started with actively praying for others in need. I believe in collective prayer and the power it has to provide peace. Giving over control to something bigger than myself makes it possible to live in the moment, which is different from how I approached things before. In the past, if

Maddie asked me to do something with her and I didn't want to, I would often do it reluctantly—unable to share her joy. I'd often become irritated with her or myself. Either way, it didn't serve me or her. I still do things I don't like to do. In fact, most of our lives are spent doing things we don't want to do. The difference for me is that I reframed the way I make commitments. If Maddie asks me to do something I don't want to do, I consider how my decision affects her. My heart may not be fully engaged, but hers is, and when we are together in it, I share in her joy. Ivey eats up time like I've never seen and I'm an incredibly impatient person. If I take her to the farmers market to pick out fruits and vegetables, she will invariably take three times longer than anyone else. Granted, she's only three. I admit there are times when I slip up and think about all the things I could be doing. Until I look at her face. Her pure joy is contagious, and I am reminded why I brought her to the market in the first place. When I look back, I know I'll never regret spending time with my girls, but I'll chastise myself if I deny them playtime or a game of catch. In the past, I was great at making excuses not to do something, but I made a conscious decision to be as selfless as possible with my family and know that giving my time reaps incredible benefits. Without excuses, there is no hiding from myself. My internal and external dialogue are aligned, and I live more authentically.

Remember this is a process, and I am constantly learning as I go. In the case of Ivey, I know I could pick out the groceries, get home, cook, and serve a meal in the time it takes her to walk over to the market and look at two stalls. But it's relinquishing control and being in the moment with integrity that makes all the differ- ence. The actually committing takes a bit of work for me too. If Jamie wants to take me on a date later in the week and I accept, I vocalize my assent to myself throughout the week. "I will go to dinner." Going to dinner isn't a burden, per se. But after days of work, practices, dance, and chores, sometimes it's difficult to mus- ter the enthusiasm to go out. Saying things out loud makes me accountable.

I get no greater pleasure than from seeing the people I love happy. It's life affirming for me and provides the impetus to give of myself even when I don't want to. Like millions of parents, we teach our children that life is about doing things we don't want to do, and if we are lucky, once in a while we get exactly what we want. Jamie and I work hard to teach our girls this philosophy during these pre- cious developmental years.

My own childhood provided a very different perspective. My parents were reared with the "Do as I say, not as I do" theory. Look- ing back, I think that's what infuriates me the most—the lack of integrity in their actions. The importance of hard work, dedication, and keeping appearances prevented any of us from speaking from our hearts and minds. We all went about our lives doing what we believed was right and let the behaviors and actions of others go unchecked. There was a huge difference between doing what we believed was right, and actually doing what *was* right. As a child, you don't know the difference. Early on, I knew something was off, but my young mind couldn't make the connection. But as I became an adult and had children of my own, I came to understand the contradiction in that approach. It was suffocating and to this day it still creates tension in the Spears family.

The cycle ends with me. I speak my mind, sometimes to the chagrin of others. When I'm unhappy or upset in a situation, I confront it the best way I can. It's something I strive to do with my family, so we don't develop deep-seated resentments and disappointments. I need to live and speak my truth. It's another way I stay accountable. It's helped me begin to heal from the challenges and disappointments in my past.

The woman I am today communicates with my parents in a way that serves me. If I don't like something that is happening, I don't keep quiet because they think it's the right thing to do. Silence goes against living authentically. I consider why I feel as I do, and what addressing the issue will do. And then I share. Sometimes speaking my truth only serves me. But more often than not, I give my parents something to think about. Pretending that everything is just fine will never serve anyone.

My approach to communicating with Jamie and our girls hopefully provides them the freedom to speak honestly about unaddressed hurts and lingering resentments. I can only speak for myself and may share a different perspective. Sometimes we are so stuck in a moment we can only see things one way. Still, there are many times when we agree to disagree. I think that's pretty normal with most families. Through action, I am trying to live my best self and encourage my own family to speak their truth.

Opening up on professional topics or addressing issues involving my family isn't so easy. There's a distinct difference between speaking on behalf of myself as compared to speaking about my family members. When I address issues as they pertain to my sister or my family, I can only speak for myself. As a family member, I am privy to experiences and information that permit me to see things differently than the general public. It's not my story to tell, nor do I have any interest in correcting media reports.

The media has made millions of dollars exposing much of my private life and that of my family. The world has a pretty good understanding of the detrimental effects of such invasive scrutiny. I experienced firsthand how destructive living life inside out can be to everyone around me. Existing this way forced my family to present ourselves to the world in a way that hid our respective inner challenges. I believe that by doing this we preserved the public's perception of Britney's persona, and we did little to protect her as a daughter and a sister or us as a family. If I'm going to break the cycle, I need to own my truth, which is the role I played in my family's life and the way I was manipulated into doing things for her that made me uncomfortable. I am culpable of so many things, but I will never claim responsibility for the challenges my sister or my family faces, nor would I ever lay blame on anyone else for my personal struggles. I love my family.

My parents' need to keep up appearances for the sake of the business has been a powerful Spears motivator since I was a toddler. I was brought into the fold and though I was given freedom and opportunity professionally, I was also expected to do whatever was necessary in support of the Britney business machine. The years I spent protecting her and being the loyal sister have been in vain. The ambiguity of her conservatorship testimonies and social media postings have left me wondering what it was all for. I miss my sister, but I can't take the blame for things I haven't done.

The world will hear many things. Some of them may be true and others may serve respective purposes. You won't hear anything from me. I have always worked hard and made conscious decisions that would lead me on my own path both personally and professionally. Like many siblings, we have our issues. But my relationship with Britney and our struggles has nothing to do with the conservatorship, but rather the boundaries I put in place to maintain the welfare of me and my immediate family. Britney's description about the way she has been managed and treated does nothing to break the cycle. All of us have to manage our lives and struggles the best way we see fit. I'm on a constant journey to balance truth with wisdom.

My approach to living my best life keeps me grounded and lets everyone see who I really am. I am the mom who always tries to put the best interests of her children first. I am the wife who shares both the privileges and challenges of sustaining a family in unprecedented times. In a time where everything you want or need to know is at your fingertips, the answers to fulfillment still lie within. At least they do for me. The things I say and do keep me authentic. Now, when I sit down to discuss a project or opportunity, my confidence and intellect infuse all aspects of the conversation. I make certain I have all the facts and convey my needs before making a decision I know will affect me as well as my family. I surround myself with insightful forward-thinkers who understand how the industry works, where it is headed, and how to make things happen. As a teen performer, I basically took opportunities that came to me without much thought. Instead of doing something simply because it is lucrative, I now consider who I am as a person, and how a given opportunity reflects the image of the woman I am today. Pursuing life authentically means I am responsible for both my successes and failures—owning the good and the bad. I am grounded and comfortable in the woman I am and plan to keep learning as I go. And after the years I spent feeling untethered, this is just the way I like it.

In Gratitude

The events of 2017 that are detailed in this book opened my eyes to the unparalleled and often overlooked heroism of first responders. Every day they perform acts of bravery and life-changing efforts during the most traumatic moments in people's lives. People like John and Victoria, EMTs from Acadian Ambulance of Louisiana, who miraculously took control of a potentially life-ending scenario and saved the life of not just one person, but that of a whole family. My family. Infinite thanks to all of the heroes who put themselves in the middle of traumas, catastrophes, and live-threatening situations to save others! We are all blessed by your service to mankind.

Acknowledgments

I am so fortunate to have this first-time opportunity to share my story with the world in a manner that feels genuine and timely. Like many of my projects, there was a team of amazing people who helped me take the thoughts and experiences of my life and transform them into a cohesive deeply personal memoir.

First and foremost, I am grateful to God and His many blessings bestowed upon me. Writing this book further highlights the ways His grace has been a guiding force in my journey.

A few years ago, I embarked on spiritual transformation that brought me to Father Mark. Thank you for being such a faithful man, for your prayers, and guiding me as I found my way back to my own faith.

In 2018, I had the distinct pleasure of being introduced to Alexis Fisher, a dynamic and discerning professional, who I connected with almost immediately. Her role as my manager has drastically changed my life by assuring me that being the authentic version of myself is enough. Alexis and the team at Timeline Management make my world go round by giving me the support I need to create the life I choose both personally and professionally. Thank you, Dina, for bringing Alexis into my life.

I am forever grateful and appreciative to Lori Balter, who listened without judgment, as I relived some of the best and worst moments of my life. She allowed me a safe place to share my truth and understood how emotional it was for me to share my story for the first time. I admire her patience with me, because I know I wouldn't have been able to put my thoughts and words on paper without having someone as talented as she is with me every step of the way.

Appreciation to the agents at Park and Fine, and the multitude of professionals at Worthy Books for their time and effort to get my story out in the world in the proper way.

I am grateful for every person who is mentioned in this book, the good and the others who may have challenged me. In one way or another, each one has made an impact that led me to where I am today.

None of this could have happened without the love and support of my husband, Jamie. Thank you for always keeping me humble, holding me accountable, but above all else, helping me break the cycle I came from.

With you, I have been able to create the family I always yearned for: a warm, loving, and stable family life that is, undoubtably, my greatest treasure.

About the Author

Jamie Lynn Spears is an actress and singer who began her entertainment career at an early age. The Louisiana native made her acting debut with a small part in *Crossroads*, portraying the fictionalized younger version of real-life sister Britney Spears's character. She then found a home in television, appearing on Nickelodeon's *All That* and most notably starring as the title character on *Zoey 101*, for which she won the Nickelodeon Kids' Choice Award for Best Actress in 2006. When she became a mother at sixteen, her pregnancy made headlines, and Spears took a six-year hiatus to focus on raising her daughter. She returned to the entertainment business as a singer who has collaborated with other artists such as Tim McGraw, Brad Paisley, and Jana Kramer. The *Zoey 101* reboot in the upcoming year is highly anticipated. She will also be coming back for the second season of Netflix's *Sweet Magnolias*.